The Military Prison
Theory, Research, and Practice

Edited by **Stanley L. Brodsky**
and **Norman E. Eggleston**

Southern Illinois University Press | *Carbondale and Edwardsville*

Feffer & Simons, Inc. | *London and Amsterdam*

COPYRIGHT © 1970, *by* Southern Illinois University Press
All rights reserved
Printed in the United States of America
Designed by Andor Braun
Standard Book Number 8093–0435–X
Library of Congress Catalog Card Number 70–103107

CONTENTS

LIST OF TABLES   *vii*

PREFACE   *ix*

NOTES ON CONTRIBUTORS   *xi*

I   Patterns in Military Corrections

1   Crime and Justice in the Military Services   *3*
STANLEY L. BRODSKY

2   Military Correctional Institutions   .   *15*
STANLEY L. BRODSKY *and*
NORMAN E. EGGLESTON

3   Military Correctional Objectives: *Social Theory, Official Policy, and Practice*   *28*
RICHARD L. HENSHEL

4   Interaction Patterns Among Military Prison Personnel   *46*
LEON D. HANKOFF

5   A Technic for Military Delinquency Management   *60*
BRUCE BUSHARD *and* ARNOLD W. DAHLGREN

6   Multidisciplinary Approach to Prisoner Rehabilitation in the Air Force   *76*
GEORGE J. BRODER

v

II   Restoration to Duty

7   Selection for Restoration, Clemency, and Parole:
An Examination of the Decision-Making Process   *91*
STANLEY L. BRODSKY

8   Characteristics of Restorees   *98*
BERNARD L. MOONEY

9   Evaluation of the Army's Restoration Program   *106*
JOHN MORRIS GRAY

III   Research Approaches

10   Role Perceptions in the Military Prison   *131*
NORMAN E. EGGLESTON

11   Mental Disease and Ability in Military Prisoners   *145*
STANLEY L. BRODSKY

12   Prisoner Evaluations of Correctional Programs   *152*
STANLEY L. BRODSKY

13   After They Leave: A Vocational Follow-Up
Study of Former Prisoners   *159*
JOHN D. NICHOLS *and* STANLEY L. BRODSKY

14   Employer Attitudes Toward Hiring Dishonor-
ably Discharged Servicemen   *170*
LEONARD J. HIPPCHEN

BIBLIOGRAPHY OF MILITARY CORRECTIONS   *183*

INDEX   *199*

LIST OF TABLES

1 Relationship of Practice, Policy, and Theory in Goals and Constraints of Army Corrections — *43*

2 Distribution of Retrainees by Major Offense Categories, 1964 — *79*

3 Psychiatric Recommendations and Return to Duty — *92*

4 Restoration Recommendations and Actions — *95*

5 Promotions and Demotions of Restorees — *119*

6 Commander Ratings of Restorees on Usefulness to Organization and Air Force or Army — *123*

7 Air Force Long-Term Success-Failure Rates, 1952–60 — *124*

8 Performance Study of Navy Prisoners Restored to Duty — *126*

9 Mean Ratings of Guards, Staff, and Prisoners Role by Guard, Staff, and Prisoner Raters — *135*

10 Critical Ratios Between Role Discrepancy Means of Sources and Subjects Rated — *136*

11 Intercorrelations Among Role Discrepancy Ratings — *137*

12 Psychiatric Diagnoses of the USDB Inmate Population from July 1941 through June 1966 — *147*

13 GTAA Percentage Distributions of Army Prisoners and Enlisted Men, 1954–65 — *149*

14 Prisoner and Staff Ratings of Institutional Programs — *154*

15 Institutional Program Ratings by Prisoners Following Differing Lengths of Confinement — *156*

16 Response Frequencies by Type of Training — *162*

17 Current Employment or Status at Time of Answering Questionnaire — *164*

18 Three Highest Ranked Factors Favorable for Hiring — *175*

19 Three Highest Ranked Factors Unfavorable for Hiring — *176*

PREFACE

The military correctional system has had an impact upon the lives of hundreds of thousands of American men in the one hundred years of its existence. The theory, goals, and applications of this system differ from civil corrections and represent an important source of information and experience in the effort to deter and modify criminal behavior. The purpose of this collection of papers is to communicate such information and experiences.

Our original plan had been to select and organize the best available articles about military corrections; however we found some major gaps in scope and coverage. As a result the first two chapters were prepared to establish a broad perspective against which the other papers and the field of study might be viewed.

The book is organized in the following sequence. The first section presents theoretical considerations and overviews of staff and institutional patterns in military corrections. The second section discusses studies related to the restoration to active duty of confined servicemen. The last section is research-oriented and focuses largely on characteristics of military prisoners.

The intended audiences are criminologists and students interested in corrections, individuals working in military and civilian settings directly related to crime and its correction, and those members of the general public who are prompted to look further into the periodically dramatic and controversial aspects of military stockades and prisons. This book is designed to serve as a resource in an important area of study in corrections, for which materials and information are not readily available. Our hope is that it will stimulate further inquiry into the military system and its implications for federal and state programs.

We wish to acknowledge the contributions of William Lyle, Jr., Anita Kuo, Thomas Lipscomb, and Annette Brodsky in editing the manuscript. The *American Journal of Correction* kindly granted permission to reprint Chapter 12. Chapter 6 appeared in *Military Medicine*. Chapters 3 and 4 appeared in the *United States Armed Forces Medical Journal,* which has since terminated publication. We appreciate the release of papers and information by the United States Disciplinary Barracks and the 3320th Retraining Group of the Air Force. Of course, the views expressed are the authors' and are not intended to represent those of either institution, of the services themselves or of the Department of Defense. Finally we are indebted to the Center for the Study of Crime, Delinquency and Corrections, Southern Illinois University, for the generous support extended in the preparation of this volume.

July 1969

Stanley L. Brodsky
Norman E. Eggleston

GEORGE J. BRODER is in private medical practice in Philadelphia. He was formerly psychiatrist, 332oth Retraining Group, United States Air Force.

STANLEY L. BRODSKY is Assistant Professor, Center for the Study of Crime, Delinquency and Corrections, and the Department of Psychology, Southern Illinois University at Carbondale. He was formerly Chief Clinical Psychologist, United States Disciplinary Barracks.

The late BRUCE BUSHARD was a Lieutenant Colonel and psychiatrist in the United States Army.

ARNOLD W. DAHLGREN is a retired Army Lieutenant Colonel. He has served as stockade confinement officer and as Deputy Commandant, United States Disciplinary Barracks. Presently he is Mill Security Chief, International Paper Company, Natchez, Mississippi.

NORMAN E. EGGLESTON is Assistant Professor, School of Social Work, University of Georgia. He is a retired Army Lieutenant Colonel and was Chief Social Worker, United States Disciplinary Barracks.

JOHN MORRIS GRAY is the Department of the Army Penologist and advises the Provost Marshal General, Department of the Army, on all matters pertaining to the Army Correction Program.

RICHARD L. HENSHEL is Assistant Professor, Department of Sociology, University of Texas. He was previously project officer for corrections with the Military Police Agency, Combat Developments Command, Department of the Army.

LEON D. HANKOFF is Clinical Associate Professor, Department of Psychiatry, State University of New York, Downstate Medical Center, Brooklyn, New York. He has served a tour of duty as a Marine division psychiatrist.

LEONARD J. HIPPCHEN is Associate Professor, Department of Criminology and Corrections, Florida State University. He formerly was Director of Research, 332oth Retraining Group, United States Air Force.

BERNARD L. MOONEY is a government psychologist in Washington, D.C. He was previously Chief Clinical Psychologist, United States Disciplinary Barracks.

JOHN D. NICHOLS is Educational Advisor in the Directorate of Training, United States Disciplinary Barracks.

The Military Prison

I

PATTERNS
IN MILITARY CORRECTIONS

Crime and Justice in the Military Services

STANLEY L. BRODSKY

> The Old Men thought and thought and at last they passed The Free Choice Law. "In order to keep Wonderfuland strong and free," they said, "every young man will henceforth be given a free choice. He can become either a soldier," they said, "or a convict."
>
> Now being a convict was the only job crumbier than being a soldier. You were shouted at, shut up and, while you weren't shot at, the pay was even lower, the hours duller, the housing drearier, the food more tasteless and the discipline stricter. Not much, but enough.
>
> So most young men, given their free choice between the two, reluctantly decided to become soldiers. They were called "heroes." And those who decided to become convicts out of moral principle or what not were called "unpatriotic punks."
>
> Arthur Hoppe,
> San Francisco *Chronicle,*
> April 3, 1969

The boundary dividing the soldier recruit and the military offender is often narrow, and their daily lives are often similar. This book is concerned with the crossing of that boundary and its consequences in the military correctional system. In this chapter we will examine military crime and justice; this includes discipline and punishment, the nature of military justice, the criminal in the service, and related research.

Discipline and Punishment

From the time when the Commander of the Roman Legion was more feared than engagement with the enemy, the military

3

services have sought to motivate soldiers through severe discipline and the principle of deterrence. Thus, Ives (1879), almost a century ago, wrote: "The repression of crime by corrective discipline depends mainly on the punishment operating widely *as an example* . . . (which) will be promoted by carrying into effect a system of discipline known to be of a severe and stringent character."

The pursuit of obedience by military services has a bloody and brutal history. In the 1189 Charter of King Richard I of England, the penalty for murder was "He who kills a man on shipboard shall be bound to the dead man and thrown into the sea" (Claver, 1954). For a substantial time in England after punishments in civilian courts became less violent, military punishments continued to be severely corporal. Boring of holes in the tongue, flagellation with the cat-o-nine-tails, branding, dismemberment, cutting off the left ear, and maiming were viewed as effective deterrents to soldiers as late as the nineteenth century (Claver, 1954).

The use of severe punishments for a deterrent effect in the military is limited neither to historical examples nor to the British services. The most dramatic recent incident in the United States was the case of Private Eddie D. Slovik (Huie, 1954), who was executed January 31, 1945, for desertion. Of over forty thousand deserters during World War II, forty-nine had been sentenced to death and only Slovik executed. The review of the convening agency in rejecting the appeal by Slovik's attorneys stated "(Private Slovik) has directly challenged the authority of the (United States), and future discipline depends on a resolute reply to this challenge. If the death penalty is ever to be imposed for desertion it should be imposed in this case, not as a punitive measure nor as retribution, but to maintain that discipline upon which alone an army can succeed against the enemy."

The traditional forms of Army discipline have given way in this century theoretically and to some degree in practice, to more enlightened approaches. Janowitz (1960) has traced to the beginning of the twentieth century this change from extreme, authoritarian discipline to a "positive discipline" based on self-reliance, psychological motivation, group affiliation and persuasion.

The early position of this positive discipline was that the military should interfere in personal matters of the soldier only when essentials related to the military are involved. This position has been subject to continuing debate. The key factors in successful use of positive group techniques in discipline, according to Baynes (1967) are the devotion, enthusiasm, and loyalty to the group with which the soldier identifies. With *esprit de corps* discipline is a natural occurrence. Without *esprit de corps* discipline is intolerable.

The Military System of Criminal Justice

Military justice is to justice, as military music is to music.
—Clemenceau

The military criminal justice system contains an intriguing and complex set of procedures. The military has its own laws, the Uniform Code of Military Justice, which exist independently of federal, state, and local criminal justice systems. Legal and police-correctional branches within the services are responsible for the implementation of this criminal justice system. Attorneys for both prosecution and defense, the military judge, as well as the court or "jury," are all drawn from the military population. All members of courts are officers and usually do not represent the peers of the defendant.

How much jurisdiction should the military have over servicemen, ex-servicemen, dependents, and military employees? In the 1950's and 1960's a series of Supreme Court decisions were directed toward limiting the historically broad judicial power of the military services. In Toth vs. Quarles (350 U.S. 11), the Supreme Court ruled that former servicemen could not be court-martialed for offenses committed while on active duty. This 1960 decision was followed in logical sequence by the 1969 O'Callahan vs. Parker decision. In the latter case the military was found not to have jurisdiction to try an army sergeant who, in civilian clothes, on pass in Honolulu, had allegedly committed housebreaking, attempted rape, and assault. The crimes for which a serviceman may be tried have been limited to service-connected offenses.

Should the Army be in the criminal justice business at all? This is a highly controversial question legally and informally. In Toth vs. Quarles the Court ruled, "Unlike courts, it is the primary business of Armys and Navys to be ready to fight war should the occasion arise. But trial of soldiers to maintain discipline is merely incidental to an Army's primary fighting function. To the extent that those responsible for performance of this primary function are diverted from it by the necessity of trying cases, the basic fighting purpose of Armys is not served."

The criminal justice system of the military has similarities to others in American society. The systems of apprehension and pretrial negotiation are not unlike those of civilian police and courts. The stockade, the first level of military confinement, resembles the city and county jail. It contains those who are in temporary detention or who have a short sentence. Some of the smaller stockades have no more facilities than the small town jail, while others have several hundred prisoners and offer a variety of rehabilitative services. The major military prisons are similar in size and construction to many large civilian prisons.

The differences between civil and military offenses, offenders, and organization of confinement facilities are quite important in the overall view of American correctional practice. Dealing with criminals and delinquents is an unsolved problem in civilian life and in the military there are complicating factors which make sound preventive and rehabilitative programs in some ways more difficult and in other respects easier to formulate and implement. In civilian life the potential lawbreaker faces the alternatives of freedom and incarceration. While the freedom may involve poverty and frustration of social aspirations, it is still more desirable than imprisonment. On the other hand, to some in the military, the role of the prisoner may be less demanding, less dangerous, and more socially and morally appropriate than the role of soldier.

Military justice and corrections have surfaced from the netherland of anonymity and respectability to the glare of considerable publicity, attention, and revision since October 1968. At that time at the Army Presidio Stockade in San Francisco, Private Richard Bunche attempted to escape and was shot and killed. Following that event, twenty-seven prisoners sat in the stockade yard, sang freedom songs, were arrested, and were charged and convicted of mutiny. Sentences initially ranged up to sixteen years at hard labor and were reduced on review to as little as one year. Two very dramatic results occurred. First, the stockade conditions and military corrections in general were publicized and criticized (Ericson, 1969). Secondly, public attention was focused on unrest in the Army and this incident was followed by a large number of other open military protests. A new class of military prisoner, the conscientious objector in the service, became prominent simultaneously.

The military's reactions to such criticisms have been historically and currently defensive. DeHart's comments in 1862 are typical; he condemned negative public opinion of military justice and prisons as corrupting to soldiers and as an evil influence to be overcome.

The Criminal in the Military Services

There are difficult methodological problems in studying the relationship between criminality and the military. The military experience is so varied for individuals in different settings that there is no single experience in which they are exposed. There are wide variations in posts, individual training, noncommissioned officers, commanding officers, morale and group process in individual companies, and situational stresses to which the individual is exposed. Depending upon the kind of sample one selects and the method he uses to study it, it is possible to conclude that the military has no effect on people who come in as criminals, that the military reforms criminals, that it corrupts non-criminals, and that the military may either be a progressive innovative, exciting possibility or a most repressive, negative influence for modifying potentially criminal behavior. The four major methodological approaches that yield these contradictory implications are:

A] The retrospective study of previous criminal histories in military offenders.

B] Observations of various samples of soldiers for "criminogenic" influences of the military services.

C] Longitudinal study of juvenile delinquents and parolees from civilian institutions in the military services.

D] Reformation of military offenders by the services themselves through restoration to duty programs.

The first three will be discussed here and restoration to duty will be considered separately in later chapters.

A. MILITARY DELINQUENCY AS A CONTINUATION
OF EARLIER PATTERNS OF OFFENDING

Retrospective studies show with great consistency that military delinquents have a higher incidence of civilian offenses than control groups. How many military offenders have been civilian delinquents? Schneider and La Grone (1945) studied five hundred rehabilitation center prisoners. They found that for three-fourths of the subjects the Army delinquency was a continuation of preservice delinquent patterns. Guttmacher and Stewart (1945) investigated 133 male AWOLS who had been referred to a psychiatric clinic. Over half had civilian convictions; this was notably higher than a control group of non-offending soldiers. Martin (1965) reported a study of 638 male military personnel who had been classified as character and behavior disorders at a psychiatric clinic and a control group of two hundred enlisted males from a non-psychiatric population. Thirty-three percent of the experimental group had previous civilian arrests, compared to 13 percent of the controls. Trenamen (1954) found that 36 percent of British offenders at a restoration center had been previously convicted in civilian life.

The motives for such offenders to enter the service seem to be heterogeneous. Shainberg (1967) conducted psychiatric interviews with fifteen hundred Navy prisoners, ages seventeen to twenty-one in the Psychiatric Department of a Naval district brig. He found five types of motives prompting these offenders to enlist: achieving confidence; accentuating alienation; becoming a good boy; attaining self glory; and group participation. His conclusion was that "the military is an unsatisfactory solution to their identity needs."

Motives for entry into the military service are often of interest in the retrospective study of military delinquency. There are four modes of entry that seem particularly common in our experience and observations.

Often enlistment occurs as a result of an alternative given by judiciary officials for the individual to be imprisoned or to enter the service. These "volunteers" with their previous histories of difficulties with the law appear prone to have difficulties with military authorities as well.

There are a substantial number of military delinquents who enlist as an impulsive act directed against a person or experience in their lives. It is a continuation of their impulsive behavior against, within, and away from the military that eventually leads to their identification as delinquent.

The phenomenon of the casual enlistment is observed in youths whose adjustment to civilian life has been marginally adequate and who report no particular motivation for entering the service. Their enlistment does not seem to represent a reaction against their environment but more part of an aimless style of life. Their expectations of the military life are vague and diffuse, and the confrontation with actual practice produces shock and feelings of inability to perform adequately.

While a great many draftees have negative feelings toward the service, most are resigned to serving as well as possible. However we have labeled as "the reluctant draftee" that type of individual who continues to resist military control of his life in a sufficiently active manner that punitive attention is directed toward him. It must be noted that there are many draftees whose methods of resistance are sufficiently passive and acceptable so that no attention is called to them.

In compiling the research on the military offender, we noted from 33 to 75 percent had been previous offenders. There are many questions left unanswered by this methodological approach. It does not reveal the percentage of individuals entering the service with civilian criminal records who were successful soldiers. It focuses only on the failures and it neglects other factors that lead to confinement.

Even among negatively motivated or aggressive individuals, there is a high degree of selectivity that precedes military imprisonment. Individuals who enter the Armed Forces undergo a screening procedure. Filtered out are most of those with ages below and above certain limits, with intelligence below certain cutoff points, with diagnosed severe mental disorders, with physical health impairment, and most with known and marked criminal records. When drafted persons are considered, then vocational, academic, and familial status may be added to the selective factors.

Once having become a serviceman, the potential military delinquent faces still more screening devices. Administrative separations are possible for individuals who cannot serve because they are "unfit" or "undesirable" for the service. Discharges without confinement under other than dishonorable conditions can be given for family hardship reasons, homosexuality, or numerous other causes. If the offender is a woman, confinement is an infrequent outcome of courts-martial.

Further alternatives to incarceration still exist once a military offense is committed. Military offenses such as being absent without leave (AWOL), disrespect to an officer, and others can be acted on locally and unilaterally by the commanding officer of the offender. The action may consist of reprimand, fine, restriction of off-duty activity, extra duty, or reduction in rank. The alleged offender may refuse to accept such a local punishment and request a court-martial.

The retrospective study approach incorporates all of these limitations. Those individuals so studied represent a very truncated sample of the total population of military offenders.

B. THE MILITARY AS A
CRIMINOGENIC INFLUENCE

Does the content of military service turn some individuals into either temporary or permanent law violators? The answer to the first part of the question is a qualified yes. Living in a military structure geared highly toward obedience, fosters violations. Actions that would not be offenses in a civilian setting become military offenses. Indeed most offenses committed in the military are not civilian offenses. Nichols (1962) reported that 92 percent of first courts-martial are for military offenses. In a World War II sample of Navy offenses, Chappell (1945) reports 94 percent as military crimes.

A variety of studies conducted in other countries support the impression that for a minority of new soldiers the experience does prompt criminal behavior in the short run where none has existed before. Thus De Smit (1964) has described a problem of recruits in peacetime as having aggression stimulated without proper outlet. Juillet (1964) studied seventy-five soldiers who had committed their first delinquent act and reported that the offenses were largely the result of adjustmental problems which vanished after a short period of time. Brickenstein (1965) suggested on the basis of six case histories that a psychiatric expert could prevent the commission of offenses through "psycho-hygienic" screening.

In an a posteriori investigation Spencer (1954) studied 283 individuals in four English penal institutions who had previously been in the service. He found that individuals who were in the maximum security prison seem to have become worse as a result of the military experience. When the effect of the military was studied for individuals in minimum security institutions and in borstals, there appeared to be little impact and previous behavior patterns were continued.

In reviewing after-effects of military service Taft (1956) has summarized, "studies have not thoroughly shown that the ex-serviceman has been disproportionately involved in crime, and those who have been so involved have not characteristically killed or assaulted their fellow Americans, but rather have stolen from them." The information on this topic is inconclusive. The actual short-term and long-term effects of military training and service remain essentially unknown and in need of careful investigation.

C. LONGITUDINAL STUDIES OF OFFENDERS:
The military as a therapeutic milieu

The most promising approach to under standing the effect of the military service on civilian criminals is longitudinal study of selected groups. The few research studies conducted longitudinally tended to use large samples and have been well designed.

Mattick (1960) studied 2,942 men from the Illinois adult prisons who had been paroled and then served in the Army. Only 5.2 percent violated their parole; 79 percent of the parolees and 91 percent of a control group made an acceptable adjustment during their Army service. In addition, when some of the parolees were followed up eight years later, a recidivism rate of 10.5 percent was found. This was less than one-sixth of the recidivism rate of parolees not in the Army. This does, not necessarily suggest that the Army prevents recidivism or repetition of criminal behavior, for there was a screening of the parolees that took place by the selective service boards. Thus, Mattick's findings may be interpreted either as the Army providing positive experiences, or the selective service boards serving as very effective screening agents.

Lejins and Tanner (1954) studied the military careers of over fourteen hundred former juvenile delinquents from two training schools in Alabama. Of these delinquents who had served during World War II and the years following, 74 percent received honorable discharges. Eighteen percent received undesirable or dishonorable discharges and were considered failures.

A longitudinal study by Roff (1956) of 470 juvenile delinquents and 828 matched controls, reported that 27 percent of the delinquents and 2 percent of the controls were rejected for moral reasons. Of those in the service, 49 percent of the delinquents and 13 percent of the controls had unsatisfactory performances.

Two year follow-ups on 134 "unsuitable" Naval recruits who were permitted to graduate recruit training and a matched control group were conducted by Plag and Arthur (1965). They reported that 72.4 percent of the unsuitables, largely character and behavior disorders, and 85.8 percent of the controls were still on active duty. The reevaluations indicated that the successful experimental subjects had emotionally matured, had experienced transitory adjustment problems during training or had been utilized in ways that called for marginal performances. No adjustmental differences between the unsuitables and the controls were present at the follow-up.

We should note that the success rates of the offenders in the Mattick, Plag, and Lejins studies are comparable to restoration success results. That is, parolees from civilian prisons, delinquents, and military restorees succeed at a rate hovering around 70 percent. The Roff data showed a notably lower success rate.

In her review of wartime induction of civilian prisoners, Cavan (1962) observed that over one hundred thousand men at one time imprisoned for felonies were inducted into the service. She suggests "from the point of view of rehabilitation of criminals, service in the Army may prove helpful to certain selected released prisoners and parolees." Thus something may occur in addition to natural maturation that helps some offenders avoid committing crimes in the military. Let us now turn our attention to the military service as a potential therapeutic milieu.

The theoretical basis for reformation of civilian offenders by the military is that of a meshing procedure. The needs of the offender mesh with the demands and presses of the service in such a way that both parties are satisfied and comfortable in the fit. Lyon (1966) suggests that the Navy supplies a consistent, virile, autocratic atmosphere that is like the lower-class gang and unlike vague, inconsistent supervision experiences in the offender's family. This concrete, masculine discipline "makes it clear (or should do so) that he *will* be accepted as a 'man' if he conforms." Such a self-concept is the object of much antisocial striving by offenders. Its attainment in a manner consonant with society's values is a positive force modifying the offender's behavior.

S. David Kahn (Gibbs, 1961) differentiates between two images of the Army that may be held by a potential offender.

If it is seen as a tough adversary, then success and self-worth are established in a test of "strength," by discharge from the service. If the Army is seen as a test of manhood, then self-worth is defined as success in making it in the Army.

Suggestions have been made for special programs in the service to resocialize the military offender. Martin (1965) discusses the military as a logical place to treat character and behavior disorders. He advises the use of hospital day programs and "primary prevention" of crimes through consultation to military units by mental health professionals.

One carefully controlled attempt to intervene in the military delinquency of first offenders was not successful. Nichols (1962) divided a sample of first court-martial offenders into one control group, one group diagnosed but not treated, and one group of seventy-seven subjects diagnosed and offered treatment. All three groups performed with equal success in follow-up studies. This one rigorous application did not support mental hygiene intervention as a recidivism prevention technique in the military. However the longitudinal research strongly points to the existence of "built-in" or automatic factors in military service that change selected offenders in positive ways.

2

Military Correctional Institutions

STANLEY L. BRODSKY *and*
NORMAN E. EGGLESTON

The military's business is fighting, defense, and protecting the national security. Why should the military services have their own prisons? And why is there a need for soldiers to become jailers?

Historically, the Army entered large-scale prison activities in 1873. At that time the United States Congress passed a bill to establish the first military prison at Rock Island Arsenal, Illinois (Henderson, 1910). When the Secretary of War protested this site because of insufficient security and possible danger to the arsenal, the original bill was amended and the military prison at Fort Leavenworth, Kansas, was established in May, 1874. The rationale has remained from that time to protect military prisoners from the bad influences and environments of state penitentiaries.

The historical development and physical structures, as well as programs and research, yield considerable information about military correctional institutions. These subjects will be considered here for stockades and brigs, Army, Air Force, and Navy institutions, staffing issues, and for restoration training.

Stockades and Brigs

Stockades and brigs are local facilities confining from two up to five hundred men. The larger stockades serve several posts or are located overseas. In cases such as the Lackland Air Force Base, Texas, stockade, joint operations are conducted by the Air Force and Army, and a moderate amount of training and treatment is provided. In other cases stockades and brigs are used exclusively as holding facilities.

Two chapters deal extensively with stockades in this book. Bushard and Dahlgren examined the large stockade at Fort Dix, New Jersey, in terms of programs introduced following a major uprising. While the results reported were positive, this article throws light on the conditions that existed before the changes. The problems of repeated deserters, unrest and manipulation among the prisoners, felt needs of the staff to be disciplinarians, and administrative inefficiency are typical of many stockades. In Hankoff's chapter, five brigs and stockades were studied. His focus was on the dynamics of stockade events and structure in both staff and prisoners. He reported that communication tended to be authoritarian from above to below, conflict existed between various enlisted men groups, and that anger toward higher authority was displaced downward to prisoners by the sentries.

A major problem in stockade operations is that stockades are controlled at local post levels. The commanding officer of the post is responsible for making basic decisions about stockades. One important result of this local control is that the stockade has low priority on the post, since military posts do not exist for the purpose of running good stockades. Indeed, some commanders see bad images of stockades as a useful deterrent to soldiers. Thus the seeking of the deterrent image plus disinterest in military corrections—except for use of prisoners in sweeping streets and packing groceries—contributes to inefficient and problem-producing stockades.

A second by-product of this local control is staffing. In many posts, stockades receive personnel drawn involuntarily from various other units. The least desirable men in the donating units are relinquished permanently and some stockades become staffed in part by misfits and unmotivated guards, rather than by individuals who can make positive contributions.

Army Correctional Institutions

The Army maximum security institution is the United States Disciplinary Barracks (USDB) at Fort Leavenworth, Kansas. Like all military prisons, the USDB shares a post with other military activities. Located near the military campus of the Army's Command and General Staff College, the tan brick front of the prison, with the black letters U.S.D.B. in relief, appears modest and small. The rest of the institution slopes downhill from the front and the wall, three feet thick and rising to a height of forty feet in places, displays numerous guard towers and floodlights. The large rectangular courtyard is framed on both sides by brick buildings painted a flesh color, and at the far end of the yard is "the castle," the central housing facility. The castle has a round core with eight wings extending from it. Four wings are used for cell blocks and the remainder for the mess hall, basketball court, office space, and other activities. Prisoners march in orderly groups through the courtyard and stroll individually, dressed in unpressed Army fatigues, dyed brown. The majority of the visible staff are military personnel, often bedecked with ribbons and other indications of service background and honors. There are two housing and living units outside the walls. A small farm houses up to forty prisoners and a new minimum security unit maintains up to 150 prisoners in several small connected buildings.

The USDB has served since 1951 as the maximum security confinement facility for both Army and Air Force prisoners. Only Air Force prisoners who are not considered for restoration to duty are sent to the USDB. There is an automatic yearly or more frequent consideration of prisoners for restoration and clemency. Prisoners who have completed one-third of their sentences and who have over a year sentence are evaluated for parole. An Army and Air Force Clemency Board acting out of Washington routinely considers all prisoners. Coughlin (1968) notes that this board's action "may consist of major surgery on a patently excessive sentence; a reduction in the sentence as an incentive or reward for continuing progress—'a carrot to nibble' so to speak; a sentence change . . . in consonance with the view of the professional staff; a change of discharge to a lesser punitive type; or where marked change has taken place in the correctional setting." These considerations and restoration to duty are positive incentives that are offered to residents of this and other military correctional facilities.

The USDB has a Research and Evaluation Council designed to promote interdisciplinary research on problems of interest to the institution and to the staff. As a result regular reports are produced, but are minimally distributed outside of the military prison. The extensive USDB vocational training program is described in the chapter by Nichols and Brodsky, who studied the training in a follow-up of released prisoners.

A second Army facility directed toward restoration training is located at Fort Riley, Kansas. This Correctional Training Facility (CTF), established in the summer of 1968, trained in ten-week cycles over nine thousand prisoners without discharges in its first year of operation. Primarily prisoners with military offenses are accepted. The training cycles are administered through a team treatment approach and the emphasis is on military skills and retraining.

Navy Correctional Institutions

The one permanent home for Naval confinement has been at the Portsmouth Naval Base, Portsmouth, New Hampshire. Since its establishment in 1908, this institution has changed names four times, beginning as the United States Naval Prison and receiving its current title of the United States Naval Disciplinary Command in 1960. One of the landmark events in the development of this Naval disciplinary facility was the command of Thomas M. Osborne at that institution beginning in November 1917. He established a "Mutual Welfare League" of prisoner self-government. The policy of this league included control and supervision by fellow prisoners; guards were relieved of all duties within the prison. Adherence to the League Constitution, voting, writing home to mothers, open reporting of news within the prison, and other innovative aspects were used as in any free, self-governing community (*The Mutual Welfare News*, 1919). This innovation lasted until 1921, during which time the prison population had varied from three hundred to twenty-three hundred. While the Mutual Welfare League was disbanded by the officer who took command in 1921, it still remains as an important penal innovation.

Since 1954, the U.S. Naval Disciplinary Command has been used as a major restoration as well as incarceration facility for the Navy and Marines. The programs, shops, and regulations are similar to those in the Army Disciplinary Barracks already described. The setting and aspects of the treatment plan are very much different, however.

To reach the Naval Disciplinary Command one crosses through the Portsmouth Naval Base, New Hampshire, until the prison appears suddenly as one turns a corner on the far end of the base. The prison itself is surrounded by an eight-foot cyclone fence that rises up and down in accordance with the whims of the rough New Hampshire countryside. The institution is dominated by a huge gray building with many gun turrets and steep towers in the central portion of the building, called "the castle." Most of the activities including inmate housing are within this building, although some industries, shops, and a chapel are in small, separate buildings.

The typical population of the prison is under one thousand. The honor company prisoners may be identified readily, since their gray uniforms are neatly pressed with blue stripes on the sides of their trousers, reminiscent of officers' uniforms in the Army. The counseling coordinator trains and supervises over one hundred part-time counselors. These counselors are enlisted men, officers, and civilians who have other jobs in the institution. Because this large segment of the staff is committed to directly helping prisoners, the typical treatment-custody dichotomy in correctional institutions is minimized.

Finally, this Navy setting provides more of a military and discipline-oriented atmosphere than either the Army or Air Force facilities. Prisoners are routinely marched to and from places within the institution, and when an officer enters a room, all of the prisoners are immediately called to attention. This emphasis on military traditional procedures extends throughout the daily activities of the Naval Disciplinary Command.

Preceding World War II this Naval prison served alone as a major facility for restoration to duty. During the war two prisons, six disciplinary barracks, two retraining commands and 375 brigs existed in the Naval confinement network (Chappell, 1945). For over sixteen years following the war the Navy maintained separate institutions for restoration training.

The Camp Elliott, California, facility bears special comment because it permitted program experimentation to study interaction between types of offenders and the nature of the institutional program (Grant & Grant, 1959). Prisoners were placed for six to nine weeks in working, closed "living groups" of twenty men with three supervisors. Offenders were classified by their maturity levels and supervisors were classified by predicted effectiveness. The criterion was restoration success of the subjects and attitude change. The supervisors predicted as effective were accepting and democratic; they produced the highest success rate with high maturity subjects. The low predicted-effectiveness supervisors were authoritarian, maximum-security guard types; they were most effective with low maturity subjects. The broad implications for corrections of these findings are being tested and implemented in the California Correctional System. The Camp Elliott approach stands as an important step in deliberate experimentation with institutional programs.

Air Force Correctional Institutions

The Air Force has been in existence for a short time as an independent military service and its correctional history is similarly short. Its crime rate is lower than the other services and it rarely has more than six hundred airmen in confinement at one time. The offenders who are seen as having little restoration potential are sent to the U.S. Disciplinary Barracks. The promising prisoners reside at the Air Force's major confinement institution, the 3320th Retraining Group at Lowry Air Force Base, Colorado. This is a small, intensive, very progressive retraining facility with less than two hundred men who are trained for periods up to six months.

The 3320th Retraining Command was located for the first fifteen years of its existence at the Amarillo Air Force Base, Texas. In 1967 it moved to Lowry Air Force Base in Denver, Colorado. Lowry Air Force Base is surrounded by two rows of barbed wire atop a six-foot chain fence. The guards at the sentry boxes seem disinterested in screening visitors and there is ready access to the base. ⁹ᵗᵉᵖ

Row after row of neatly landscaped white barracks on the base display thirty-foot-high brick chimneys, and each small group of buildings bears a four-digit identification. The 3443rd Squadron is followed in the next block by rows of one-story and two-story buildings, inconspicuously displaying a coat of arms and "3320th Retraining Group."

The one hundred and fifty staff members, including thirty enlisted counselors, in part are organized into multidisciplinary teams. Three to four staff teams have been operating since the early 1960's and replaced classification boards in the group. A discussion of the *modus operandi* of the teams and the group overall is presented in Broder's chapter about the 3320th Retraining Group. This Air Force group has been cited as a positive example of military corrections offering a therapeutic community for offenders (Johnson, 1968).

A major emphasis in organization and activities in the 3320th Retraining Group is research. The group utilizes full-time researchers studying, among other things, group processes, success rates and team functioning. Follow-ups on success rates in restoration range from 60 to 80 percent for group retrainees. An example of group research that has policy implications is presented in Hippchen's chapter. His survey of businesses of varying sizes and types reported the positive and negative factors affecting employment of discharged Air Force offenders. The need to open communication channels between industry, the offender, and the penal institution are often discussed. The study by Hippchen is one of the few efforts to present empirical data on this important subject matter.

Staffing

The staffing at military correctional institutions consists of military career personnel at the upper and middle management levels, enlisted personnel at the guard level, and civilians in vocational training and various administrative posts. The major object of attention has been the guard or sentry. Hankoff's chapter observes the very powerful stresses placed on the sentry in the brig. Simons (1963) reported two case studies of stockade guards whose adjustmental patterns prior to working in the stockade were successful. They suffered acute adjustmental problems, experiencing impending sadism and an acute paranoid attack, respectively, following placement in the guard role.

Brodsky and Grossheim (1965) have discussed the need for prescreening the kinds of individuals who become guards. They suggest that there is a need for mental-hygiene teams to eliminate those likely to respond with inappropriate behavior patterns before such guards get into positions of power or difficulty. Von Holden and Isenstadt (1969) have suggested that the name "guard" itself promotes difficulty in being effective as rehabilitation agents. Many civilian institutions have discarded this job description and they suggest that the titles custodial or correctional technicians would enhance the activities, roles, and rehabilitative potential of military guards.

One theory emphasizing the need for positive staff is based on modeling. That is, trainees or prisoners tend to model their behavior after the staff. A staff member who presents a healthy, mature model will produce the same behavior traits in prisoners. Eggleston's chapter suggests that prisoners differentiate between guards and other staff very sharply in terms of satisfaction. In the Grant and Grant (1959) Camp Elliott study, this was not supported. The most effective results in restoration success occurred when staff and prisoners levels of maturity coincided, rather than high effectiveness-maturity staff uniformly promoting greater success with all trainees.

Hymes and Blackman (1965) sought to study the staff variable in five training regiments at Fort Dix, New Jersey. This basic-training camp had thirty-three hundred trainees and about six hundred cadres at the time of the study. To see if cadre did indeed act as models for the trainees, they studied the offense rates and the rates of savings bond purchases of the cadre and trainees in each of these five regiments. They found low, but significant Spearman rank-order correlations of $+.24$ to $+.29$ between cadre and trainee offenses, depending on the offense type. However, they found a much higher and significant rank-order correlation of $+.72$ between cadre and trainee savings bond participation. They concluded, as we do, that the atmosphere set by the individuals in command does indeed affect the behavior of the trainees. The precise cause-and-effect relationships have yet to be fully understood.

Restoration to Duty: the Military Retraining of the Military Criminal

In disciplining its delinquents the military services may exercise an option that has no equivalent in civilian life. An individual may be sentenced without a discharge so that he automatically returns to active military duty following his incarceration. In addition, the military considers a discharged offender for possible return to duty during the time he is confined. This capability of casting out and taking back provides an unusual flexibility which will be dealt with here and in separate chapters on restoration to active duty.

The status of the military prisoner is an extraordinary one. He has very recently left the peer group of his guards and, in the case of over one-fourth of the prisoners, will soon be rejoining this group without official bias. Because the soldier in confinement in many cases is expected to return to active duty, there is a qualitative difference between military and civilian perceptions of the prisoner. Many civilian prisons treat their charges as outcasts and fail operationally to acknowledge that the prisoner has come from and will return to the society which includes the staff; in the military prison there appears to be a closer identification with the prisoner by staff. He retains his status as an *errant soldier*.

The emotional meaning of the prisoner's status as *errant soldier* can involve both positive and negative reactions. For some career soldiers who are strongly identified with the Army, the rejection of the Army implies rejection of patriotic duty and, more specifically, rejection of the value system of the career soldier. The guards or other staff members sometimes overreact and become punitive in treatment of the inmate.

On the positive side, the status of *errant soldier* reduces the social distance between staff and inmate. For those of higher rank and longer experience in the institution, we observe more of the traditional military pattern of relating to subordinates in a paternalistic manner. For the younger, lower ranking staff who are newly assigned, there is a more threatening and fluctuating pattern of identification with the prisoner who is so similar to himself, with phases of rejection and overidentification.

One of the important goals of the military confinement system is identical in many cases with the prisoner goals: that of restoration to honorable duty. Even some prisoners who have deliberately and repeatedly deserted, find that the consequences of their acts away from the precipitating situation elicit a desire to return to duty. This goal of restoration to active military duty represents an outcome from imprisonment that is different from goals in civilian penal institutions. There are five very distinctive features about return to military service as an outcome.

Most goals set upon release from civilian settings are long-term aims that require planning, organizing, sustained effort, and obstacles with which the ex-prisoner has had prior difficulty. Becoming a soldier again permits the individual to return immediately as a success and his confinement behavior has a direct consequence in his disposition with regard to restoration.

The military uniform and return to the active combat unit are specific, demonstrable proof of goal attainment. The soldier is there, serving on duty, carrying a weapon—he has these very concretely defined and accepted signs of success.

The commonly defined measure of success in studies of civilian prisoners has been the avoidance of further confinement. In the case of the military, the goal is positive. Rather than staying out of prison or avoiding courts-martial, it is serving as a successful soldier.

The restoree has the opportunity to participate in the activity of being in the Army, with its patriotic halo effect, and presumably is contributing to his nation's well-being.

The military nature of the prison, with enlisted men and officers serving as guards and staff, has a potentially powerful motivational and identification-producing effect. The individuals restored, as noted, will be going back into the same group to which their keepers belong. The guard knows that the prisoner potentially is going back to the service and that he may be serving at the same post, drinking at the same service club, and eating in the same mess hall. In turn, the prisoner has as his models for behavior people who are a sample of those to whom he will return. These are successful individuals—not as guards or jailers or keepers—but as soldiers, and as such are models for the successfully returning soldier.

THE BRITISH EXPERIENCE

During and following World War II the British Army instituted several programs for retraining its military delinquents. The rationale bears a great similarity to that described in the American military forces. That is, they were designed "with a view to reclaiming young soldiers from a career of crime and converting them into good soldiers" (Trenaman, 1952).

Trenaman reports that during the Second World War three different sites were used for these Special Training Units (S.T.U.) for restoration. In one sample studied by Trenaman, 76 percent of 696 retrainees were returned to fighting units in the field. In three-month follow-ups, less than 25 percent of the returnees were given below-average or bad ratings by their commanding officers. Seventy percent received honorable discharges and on release ratings, 53.6 percent received satisfactory evaluations. This high incidence of success was achieved in the face of imposing personality problems of the subjects. Trenaman notes "the great majority of the S.T.U. population were found to have deep-seated problems which seemed likely to bring them into conflict with any authority, service, or civilian."

Spencer (1954) observed that there were nine military confinement facilities in Great Britain during the Second World War and by 1947 they had been divided into two types of military prisons. Type A, for recidivists, was operated like any good civilian prison, and conducted no military retraining. Type B, the Military Corrective Establishment (M.C.E.), was designed for retraining of capable offenders for restoration. The M.C.E. at Colchester used three stages of training, accompanied by increasing freedom, and was operated much like the 3320th Retraining Group of the Air Force.

THE UNITED STATES EXPERIENCE

The chapter by Gray discusses in detail the Army, Navy, and Air Force experiences with restoration to duty. Gray reports a 71 percent success rate in the Army. Von Holden and Kroll (1968), in a study of 305 prisoners restored to military duty from the U.S. Disciplinary Barracks, found that 60.7 percent were successful at the end of a six-month follow-up. There were 56.5 percent successes among those who had been sentenced without a discharge. There was an 84.4 percent success rate among those who had been sentenced with a punitive discharge. Similarly Dixon (1963) had reported the success rate of Air Force restorees to be 59.2 percent for those without punitive discharges and 70.2 percent for those with discharges. This differential rate reflects at least two factors. One, much more careful screening for restoration to duty occurs with those who have punitive discharges; two, there is a higher motivation among those restored with punitive discharges to remove the stigma of the military conviction.

Summary

As military confinement historically replaced corporal punishment of the potential military offender, a variety of positive approaches and correctional innovations have developed. The physical structures of military correctional institutions range from high-walled dungeons and fortresses to unfenced barracks. The psychological settings similarly range from traditional maximum-security milieus to therapeutic communities.

There is no single, predictable experience for offenders in military confinement. The nature of the experience is a function of the service and the particular institution. If a service delinquent had a broad perspective, was cunning, and wanted to get the maximum benefit from military confinement, the present review suggests a course of action; he should commit an offense just serious enough to keep him out of the stockade and just mild enough to qualify him for restoration training.

3

Military Correctional Objectives: Social Theory, Official Policy, and Practice

RICHARD L. HENSHEL

The Need for Analysis

The Army's correctional policy since its inception weaves a long path from the Adjutant General's Office to the Judge Advocate General to the Adjutant General again and finally to the Provost Marshal General. The vast fluctuations in the size of its prisoner population were far in excess of expansion and contraction of the Army. Most importantly as one reviews the quoted speeches, writings, and public relations efforts of the persons responsible for the program, through all of this one central impression stands out. Fortunately or unfortunately, by unstated design or by accident, the impression emerges that the Army's correctional "program" has developed as a result more of pushes and pulls from external pressures than as an internally generated product of coherent rational planning to meet certain objectives. As a result, it has often produced a "hodge-podge" of policy, just as do all "systems" created largely by *compromises between conflicting external pressures*. Of course no program in any organization the size of the Army (in fact no program anywhere) exists without the unpleasant necessity of compromising with other competing goals or objectives. Still, some aspects of the Army have been relatively more powerful than others, and it is in this relative sense that the writer refers to the long-term powerlessness of corrections vis-à-vis other systems which impinge or interface with it.

The writer should like to offer below what he considers the central reason for this problem. It is a simple one: corrections has not lacked for concerned individuals; rather its weakness lies in an inability among those responsible to agree on the goals of corrections. As usually stated, this is seen as a conflict between the "hard noses" and the "reformers," however something more will be said about the inadequacy of this typology below.

Symptomatic of the whole problem has been its compounding by extraordinary language difficulties. "Punishment," for instance, which is manifestly a feature of Army corrections—whether intended so or not—is an unmentionable today, so much so that this writer was tempted to invent a euphemism, "programmed unpleasantness" or some such, when it became time to refer to it. "Discipline," however, as in "Disciplinary Barracks," is slightly more acceptable in dealing with Army corrections, but is not in favor. "Correction" is a good word: witness the "Army Correctional Program." Today, the term "rehabilitation" is in vogue. In addition, facilities change their names, as if by this means to better achieve the goals of corrections. The old United States Military Prison became the United States Disciplinary Barracks; the guardhouse the stockade; the Rehabilitation Centers of World War II the Rehabilitation Training Centers of today and the Correctional Training Facilities of tomorrow. All of which is not to say that policies in these facilities did not improve—indeed they did—but merely to point out, via the examples in this paragraph, first the degree to which improvement has often been "linguistic" rather than factual, and second to underscore the high level of "lip service" that has emerged.

Lip service of a sort is to be found in all organizational structures, as an inescapable result of the fact that no organization can entirely live up to its ideals which it nevertheless feels required to reiterate. But organizations and programs can and do vary markedly in the extent, the pervasiveness of that lip service, and it is here, as another symptom of the problem, that the philosophical foundations of Army corrections unfortunately become noticeable. Everyone from the casual prisoner through the custodial personnel to the confinement officer and higher knows, for example, that punishment is a prominent feature of stockade existence, and that rehabilitation as a programmed feature is virtually nonexistent. New officers and custodial personnel go through an elaborate social training process in which they learn first to successfully state the correctional philosophy and then, by observation, reading between the lines, or off-the-record remarks by experienced personnel, to disregard this for the most part and get on to the nitty-gritty of custody and control, of postage stamps, and sentence computations. The philosophy is something to be learned; something to have ready for recitation at the proper moment; it is not something to interfere with the day-to-day workings of the facility. The picture thus far painted is not wholly or everywhere true, of course, but it is accurate to a very uncomfortable extent.

The above paragraphs at first seem unduly harsh toward the Army corrections program, but they should be taken in proper perspective. The real achievements of Army corrections should not be forgotten. The intent here is not to ridicule the program but, by using the above items as "symptoms," to point out what seems to have historically been the root of the problem in corrections. The personnel in the Army deeply concerned with corrections have been split among themselves regarding just what confinement, parole, clemency, and so forth can and should accomplish. In addition, more peripheral but equally powerful figures in the shaping of military correctional philosophy and policy have also been split among themselves. However, it is the split in the former which seems most important. In an organization the size of the Army, an area of concern like corrections can only become a center of decision—i.e., relatively autonomous—if the persons responsible are in concert about what it should accomplish. If, as seems to have been the case with corrections, its advocates are scattered among several branches (Adjutant General, Judge Advocate General, and Military Police), each of which tends to see the problem in a somewhat different light, and if even within a branch there remains fundamental (if often unspoken) disagreement over very basic objectives, then the area will almost assuredly become a "football" of other centers of decision, and will have its legal, personnel, training, funding, and facilities problems decided for it in relation to other problems. This is especially true when the area is relatively peripheral to the Army's central missions and when the number of persons involved is few.

The above is not a plea for the supremacy of corrections in the framework of Army planning. By its very nature the field of corrections is, as stated, peripheral to the central Army missions, and as such cannot reasonably expect to override the most fundamental policy decisions. On the other hand, when one considers the critical importance of discipline, law, and order, which should be intimately tied-in to corrections due to the deterrent effect of confinement, and when, in addition, one considers the "salvage" problem of those who have already violated military order in terms of "rehabilitation" versus the cost of training a replacement, then it begins to be apparent that the corrections policy as implemented is no trifling matter. How many prisoners, just to take one quick example, have become rehabilitated through performing their post's garbage collection? The answer might surprise us: perhaps a few have. Yet nowhere in the evolution of the standard practice of employing prisoners on the menial tasks of an installation was consideration given to the costs of garbage collection, say, versus the costs of training a replacement for the man. As another quick example, consider the case of "Christmas clemency" (as distinguished from regular clemency) in which prisoners may be released who are not yet ready for the step in a short-sighted form of Christmas spirit. Clearly, in many instances corrections as actually operated has been a case of the tail wagging the dog. Corrections should be a generating center of policy decisions and not a function often preempted in practice by demands of objectivity in less important areas.

It seems to the writer that in order for military correctional policy to develop (and be implemented in practice) as a product of coherent, rational planning, meeting all of its objectives as far as possible, that the goals which corrections should aim for must first be set forth explicitly and agreed upon. This feeling is held for the following reasons: First, because as stated above corrections can never become a generator of decisions in the Army until the scattered individuals responsible for it agree at least to a considerable extent on what it should be accomplishing. Second, because in order to justify increases in funds, manpower, training, improvements in personnel policies, and so forth, a coherent set of objectives that these changes will meet must be specified. Third, because unless we agree on what corrections should be doing there is no way to measure how successful it is (in short, evaluation), and without measures of relative success or failure it becomes virtually impossible to justify any changes that go contrary to good old "common sense."

Because of this sense of urgency, the writer has intrepidly entered the hornet's nest. In the section to follow he will try to outline the goals of military corrections. But what reasons have we to expect any tangible success now given the long history of the problem? Two things have seemed important here. First must be the surprising lack of effort to examine the basic goals of corrections. Many of the best brains in this area are deeply concerned with the relative advantages of different operating policies, with training and facilities and so forth. Not to belittle such problems at all, "just what are we trying to achieve with our correctional program?" will draw more than the normal share of blank looks. But this important question, not at all rhetorical, is usually passed over in favor of consideration of operational decisions that actually depend upon it. A second factor might be termed the "single goal syndrome." Too often when the problem of fundamental goals is, at last, considered, it is seen as essential to pick out one and only one. For example, the goal (singular) of Army confinement is often stated as correction of the offender, not punishment. A multi-goal state for military corrections is all too rarely considered. But this too is a most serious question: can the ends of corrections really be contained within the confines of a single objective? The writer believes not, and feels this to be a central problem in setting up military correctional policy, *for covert or concealed goals are usually incorporated to some extent, yet rarely examined.* An "either-or syndrome" follows from the setting of single goals, and results in the typing of correctional leaders as either "hard noses" or "reformers." Not only does more than one goal seem necessary, but the several goals in fact "conflict" with each other to a certain extent, and this factor may be at the bottom of the "syndromes." Yet all of the goals seem equally essential.

In any event the establishment of the goals of Army corrections seems too essential a task to forfeit without the attempt, the long history of the problem notwithstanding.

The Goals of Corrections

Our first step in attempting to set down a series of goals for Army corrections might be to investigate what other theorists have maintained in the past. Literature on the problem is certainly far from lacking. But philosophies of law differ among themselves regarding the number, description, and priority of correctional objectives. In addition virtually all of the prominent theorists were writing with civil corrections in view, and corrections in the military appear to present several basic problems not commonly found elsewhere, some of which will be touched upon below. At any rate, while the objectives offered below undoubtedly owe a great deal to civil theories, it has seemed best to create a solution specifically to meet the military situation.

Before initiating discussion of the objectives themselves a word of caution about the terminology employed is in order. The terms "basic objective," "derived objective," and "constraints" have been used with respect to the objectives set forth. The employment of these terms is admittedly on an intuitive basis, although the author would maintain that some logic is involved, and no claim to strict mathematical or logical 'derivation" is being made.

Let us begin, then, with the "basic objective" of military corrections. In the writer's frame of reference this must be:

BASIC OBJECTIVE:
The protection of military and civil order

It should be noted that this basic goal is fundamental to other areas of interest besides corrections—the preventative enforcement task of the Military Police to mention only one example. It is essential, however, to specify the basic objective because it occasionally becomes possible for derived objectives to subvert this basic goal unintentionally while appearing only to perform their own functions more intensively.

There are two basic means which have historically been used throughout the society as a whole to protect the civic order. These might be termed the "inner-directed" approach and the external, reward-punishment approach. In the former, a conscious effort is made to inculcate within the individual certain values, orientations, outlooks on life and institutions, which will create an internal need for the adoption of desired modes of behavior. At least a minimum of this path must be used, since it is totally impossible to police everyone's actions all of the time, and therefore a substantial amount of "self" regulation is necessary. In the Army this is handled largely through reliance upon influences which the person experienced prior to entering the service. "Character guidance" supplements this background. The second approach is also necessary, since no matter how successful for the most part the inculcation of desired values may be, there will always be some people who cannot be reached in this way. In addition, special situations of unique temptation may arise even for persons who have been reached. For these reasons, an "external" reward-punishment path is a necessity, in which the actions of persons are observed and gratification or deprivation meted out accordingly. In the Army this can take the form of promotion, decoration, commendation, reprimand, et cetera.

Although the exact means of applying the two methods may vary widely for the reasons noted above it does not seem possible for a social order to survive without some reliance upon each.

Turning now to the area of corrections in particular, we are here dealing with proven violators of the Army's legal order. The two above approaches to protection of order are reflected in the treatment of these "failures" in two ways.

1. DERIVED OBJECTIVE: *The deterrence of future violations through observable punishment of the offender.*

This is the necessary reflection of the external reward-punishment path mentioned above. Its objective is to render the life of the offender unpleasant in some significant way. In the Army correctional program at the present time this is accomplished through *1*] deprivation of freedoms and rigid control over the prisoner's daily existence; *2*] denial of alcoholic and sexual gratifications; *3*] lengthy work schedule, often at menial or unpleasant tasks. While the exact mechanisms may vary widely, the goals of the deterrent objective are twofold: first, to serve as a "warning" to others of the unpleasant consequences of proscribed actions, and second, to deter the prisoner himself from future acts after his release.

It is often pointed out that swiftness and certainty of punishment are more important in the creation of a deterrent effort than the magnitude of the punishment itself. The writer has no quarrel with this—in fact he agrees with it—so long as this is not taken to mean that the magnitude of punishment can be ignored, or that punishment can be abolished entirely in favor of rehabilitation. Such a system would only remain effective so long as persons on the outside subject to temptations were unaware of the correctional system's true nature.

Returning to the means of maintaining social order, we recall that the "internal" control has not yet been covered. Since offenders are, by definition, persons in whom both internal and external controls have broken down, it follows (unless the individuals are to be incarcerated for good) that upon his release a prisoner must either be watched extremely closely—in order for the "external" controls to be effective— or, preferably, while in confinement be reformed (rehabilitated, converted) in terms of his orientation toward society, so that extensive post-release surveillance becomes unnecessary. When the latter is the case, the prisoner may be profitably reabsorbed into the military community upon his release, eliminating manpower and training replacement requirements.

Thus the "internal" means of social control is reflected in the treatment of offenders through:

2. DERIVED OBJECTIVE: *The reformation,
in terms of genuine attitude change,
of the military prisoner.*

Outside of the Disciplinary Barracks at Fort Leavenworth, the home of the more serious military offender, reformation in the present Army correctional program is attempted through the mechanisms of religious attendance and guidance, "character guidance," individual counseling, a limited-skill development program, and voluntary educational programs. It seems a general consensus that, unfortunately, the level of reformation actually accomplished is minimal. While much of this problem might be laid to the short stay of most stockade offenders (at a sampled facility it averages forty days), the reasons which the writer believes most essential will be discussed below.

Having now set forth above the basic objective and its two "derived" approaches, let us now examine several necessary "constraints" upon the military correctional system. These constraints are unavoidable, inherent limitations on the accomplishment of the objectives heretofore outlined. To begin with:

CONSTRAINT:
*Elaborate security systems must
be established to maintain custody and
control of the offender*

Most of the "treatments" which may be imposed for violations of the Army's legal code are unpleasant to the offender. This includes both measures punitive per se and measures reformative, for by reformation the writer does not refer to idyllic situations in contrast to deterrence but to actual reformation, and most recorded experience has shown that situations producing genuine attitude change are themselves somewhat stressful and unpleasant. Assuming that most prisoners subjectively regard their situation as unpleasant, the Army will be forced to deal with efforts of the violator to avoid the treatment. These efforts may take many forms (e.g., legal subterfuge), but we will here concentrate upon two: attempts by the prisoner to physically absent himself from the place or places of correction, and, within these places, to upset the planned treatments which he dislikes. These tendencies on the part of the prisoner require corresponding measures on the part of his captors—to wit: custody and control respectively. The methods employed to secure and control have a way of "running away" with the correctional program and of subverting the basic objectives, as will be set forth in greater detail below.

CONSTRAINT:
The correctional program must be "economical" in funds and manpower

This is one of those "needless to say" provisos which, in practice, prove very difficult to define. Consider the question of prisoner labor, dealt with briefly above. Menial tasks on an installation have to be accomplished beyond a doubt, but by all accounts prisoner labor is the most inefficient means possible. When the armed guard is included it becomes a moot point whether the labor is "profitable" at all, especially in terms of the probable degradation of reformation which results thereby. Unfortunately, no study of the economic aspects of military prisoner labor exists, to the writer's knowledge. To take another elusive aspect of economics, since the prisoner is considered to require elaborate and expensive precautions to insure his physical custody, the practice has traditionally been to bring prisoners together in stockades, guardhouses, or whatever, so that a maximum of prisoners can be watched at a minimum of cost. But if real reformation as a goal is placed in the picture the cost problem becomes much more complicated. For what happens when all prisoners are placed together in a confinement facility—prisoner segregation notwithstanding—is that we take the "bad apples" in the Army and put them *together* where they can influence one another and mutually reinforce the very same ideas and outlooks that got them into trouble in the first place. This "prisonization" or prison socialization does much to nullify any reformation efforts made, and in fact the offender may leave the facility more pronounced in his antisocial orientation than when he entered. Thus the economics of correctional facilities of various sizes, modes of segregation, and so forth becomes far more complicated than the mere consideration of physical plant and guard force. "Economical," in short, becomes a very difficult term to define in practice, one which requires far more statistical support than is currently being collected.

CONSTRAINT:

Facilities for combat-zone cases must be sufficiently unattractive to discourage voluntary entrance

So far we have been considering objectives and constraints which in many respects are indistinguishable from those of many civilian programs. The mission of the Army, however, and its means of executing it in terms of land combat, yield an additional constraint not ordinarily a factor elsewhere. This factor is that conditions on the front (or "in action," to include Vietnam) are so physically miserable and dangerous, as everyone will admit, that what in other circumstances would be regarded as punishment or unpleasant might be taken by a soldier serving under these conditions as an improvement over his present state. A confinement facility, for instance, at least serves hot meals, offers freedom from fear of death, and so forth. In the vast majority of cases, of course, the "internal" motivation referred to earlier proves sufficient to overcome such a comparison. Frontline service is honorable, the stockade is not. Indeed most frontline observers report an increase in this internal self-sacrificing motivation. Nevertheless the Army has also traditionally had to deal with the problem of the malingerer, and the problem might grow much more acute if the confinement facility were too attractive. For this reason, to prevent large-scale "voluntary" entrance into the correctional system, a facility servicing combat-zone prisoners cannot present too appealing an appearance.

Civilian facilities, on the other hand, usually need not contend with this problem, since an ordinary institution represents a harsher environment than does the "outside." (An exception is occasionally found in the "revolving door" drunk, but he is such a small part of civilian corrections that special pains are not needed to deal with his unusual contentment.) This increase in harshness is also true for garrison military prisoners, and even prisoners from the communications-zone behind the front. The constraint therefore appears primarily a concern when dealing with combat-zone cases.

A Recapitulation

BASIC OBJECTIVE:
The protection of military and civil order

DERIVED OBJECTIVE: The *deterrence* of future violations through observable punishment of the offender.

DERIVED OBJECTIVE: The *reformation,* in terms of genuine attitude change, of the military prisoner.

CONSTRAINT: Elaborate security systems to maintain *custody and control* of the offender.

CONSTRAINT: The correctional program made *"economical"* in funds and manpower.

CONSTRAINT:* Facilities for combat-zone cases made sufficiently unattractive to discourage voluntary entrance.

"Conflicting" Goals

As mentioned earlier, some of the goals of corrections "conflict" with one another to some extent, and this conflict or strain may be at the bottom of the "single goal" and "either-or" perspectives. Some of the conflicts have already been encountered in the discussion of the economic constraint, in which it was pointed out that fulfillment of the deterrent objective leads to increased costs due to the prisoner's heightened desire to escape, and that the accomplishment of cost reduction by placing prisoners in a confinement facility leads to increased difficulty with rehabilitation efforts. Economy in the operation of a correctional facility (although probably not economy in the broader sense) also is in conflict with rehabilitation, considering the costs of training a professionalized staff, and the cost of additional staff members. Finally economy is in conflict with custody and control, since it costs money and manpower to increase guard forces and improve physical facilities.

So much is fairly obvious, but now let us consider some strains less immediately apparent. To begin with, deterrence is often in direct conflict with rehabilitation. There are several reasons for this. To begin with, while it is not impossible by any means for a person to accept and "internalize" advice from someone he sees as hurting him, a very special type of relationship is called for before this can occur. The reason for this, evidently, is that it is hard for a man to accept the fact that a person who is hurting him in one sense is actually trying to help him (rather than just "doing his job") in another sense. Incidentally it is also hard to convince the staff member of this too. Usually, therefore, the orientation and advice given in this situation has far less effect (except perhaps for immediate visible compliance) than orientation and advice given by nonpunishing persons—in this case, unfortunately, the man's fellow prisoners. The more unpleasant the man's state (again with exceptions), the harder it becomes to convince him that a counselor really has his best interests at heart. In addition, even if the man in confinement does become convinced that a counselor is concerned, he still generally feels a certain hostility toward the "institution" itself, and, particularly significant here, its stated goals. Since he ordinarily is unconvinced of the justice of his situation, he retaliates against the institution in one of the few ways left open to him: he refuses to become "brainwashed." Here at last we can speak from concrete evidence: data from surveys conducted across several civil prisons has revealed that the extent of prisoner attitude change varies inversely with the punitive character of the facility. Hence, as we increase deterrence—at least in its punishment aspect—we interfere more and more with reformation. Yet deterrence remains a necessity.

Similarly, the unpleasantness limitation on combat-zone prisoners conflicts with rehabilitation. The reason for this is that the physical discomforts in a confinement facility are not viewed by prisoners in the same way as the physical limitations of combat. This is because the prisoner takes into account *intentionality*. In combat, physical discomfort is usually viewed as an unavoidable phenomenon; whereas in confinement it is seen as avoidable and as stemming from the intent of the captors. Thus whether it is called punishment or not it is seen as punishment, and conflicts with reformation in a way identical with the conflict between punishment and reformation.

Finally, the requirement of custody and control interferes with rehabilitation. This interference comes from two sources, the first of which—prisonization—has already been mentioned. The remaining cause stems from the fact that stringent custody control measures are viewed as punishment by the prisoner, because of the same factor of intentionality mentioned above, and thus conflict with rehabilitation as outlined.

The Present System

The points just covered regarding strains between the goals of corrections are not merely elements in a pedantic exercise: they enable us to obtain, first, a pretty good view of why the "single-goal" and "either-or" perspectives arise. They also allow us to see certain limitations *inherent* in the design of correctional systems. Finally they allow us a "handle" on an analysis of the condition of the present correctional system, the topic of this brief section.

At the present time, the official Army correctional policy as stated by the Department of the Army and Department of Defense is quite specifically reformation-oriented. Punishment is virtually unmentionable in today's official regulations and literature, undoubtedly deriving in large part from the reputation for brutality of the old military prisons. Punishment in some form nevertheless seems to the writer an unfortunate necessity in any workable deterrent design, and indeed how can a prisoner be sentenced to a stockade as punishment unless there is something unpleasant involved in being there?*

While rehabilitation is the stated goal, no one seems to know quite how to achieve it. Conceptions usually revolve around minor improvements in the present system, which most concerned officers regard as largely ineffective. But, meanwhile, the means of achieving custody and control are understood. In addition few working models of effective rehabilitation programs (for example the Provo and Highlands experimental projects) are found, while models of correctional systems built largely around custody and control are widespread. These problems render both the creation and the day-to-day management of a real rehabilitation program even more difficult. Thus a tendency to develop a program centered around custody and control is found, despite stated policy.

In addition, it is very difficult, although not impossible, to *measure* the effectiveness of rehabilitation, while this is easy to do for custody and control (number of escapes, parole violations, etc.). No attempt is made at present to measure stockade rehabilitation effectiveness. This is one other cause (and perhaps result as well) in what appears to be the objective downplay of rehabilitation and the reinforcement of custody and control.

Finally, then, we have the following situation: punishment is an unmentionable, yet is widely felt to be essential. Custody/control, meanwhile is at once an acceptable discussion topic, well understood and easily measured. What seems to happen then is that *punishment is carried out covertly through the imposition of measures which are ostensibly for custody and control.* (The writer does not necessarily object to this, in fact it may be a workable approach but it should be recognized.) The odd fact of the matter is thus that rehabilitation, the stated policy of Army corrections, is virtually nonexistent in the stockade, yet the fact remains undiscovered—except in the uneasy suspicions of many concerned officers—due to lack of measure-

---

* An old Army saw states that a prisoner "is sent to the stockade *as* punishment not *for* punishment"—to purportedly show the non-punitive nature of stockade existence.

ment of rehabilitation under the present statistical system. Instead, meanwhile, the present program can only be described as primarily oriented around custody and control.

The Future or Where Do We Go from Here?

It might be advantageous at this point to stop and consider the relation between practice, policy, and theory on each of the goals and constraints set forth. Accordingly, in Table 1 a display of this relationship has been constructed.

1. Relationship of Practice, Policy, and Theory in Goals and Constraints of Army Corrections

	Constraints		
Item	Present Practice	Army DoD Policy	Corrections Goal Theory
Reformation	No	Yes	Yes
Punishment	Yes	No	Yes
Custody/Control	Yes	Yes	Yes
Economy	Questionable	Yes	Yes
Discourages Voluntary Entrance	Yes	Not stated	Yes

The relationship with respect to punishment is especially interesting. Official policy states that punishment is non-desirable and not practiced; the writer maintains that it is necessary and is practiced. Taken either way, the Army appears to be doing the right thing. The chief weakness pinpointed in the display is, as usual, the lack of rehabilitation in practice.

The stated purpose of this article is not to set forth a program for military corrections, but merely to analyze the present system and set down goals for the future. Nevertheless some programmatic comments are not entirely out of order.

1] When one examines the goals and constraints as set down above, it is obvious that no one single goal adequately encompasses the aims of a viable correctional program. If, for public relations reasons, official Army doctrine does not acknowledge one or more of the objectives mentioned, this is one thing; it is another thing for responsible individuals themselves to be unaware of the reality. Neither of the two derived goals are paramount, but both appear necessary. All indications (nonstatistical, unfortunately) point to an inadequacy in the reformation goal as currently implemented. Custody and control, on the other hand, not a goal at all but a constraint on the real goals, has tended to "run away" with the program, and to become a covert means of punishment. This is not necessarily worse than another form of punishment, and indeed may be more politically acceptable than most, but it is important that the matter be recognized.

2] If rehabilitation is truly to be implemented, then it is patent that some system to *measure* rehabilitation—however imperfect it may necessarily be—is essential. The Air Force attempts to measure the effectiveness of its experimental 3320th Retraining Group, and the Disciplinary Barracks does the same, but there is virtually no follow-through elsewhere in the Army's correctional program. Several methods are possible, but this is not the time to mention them. One or a combination of methods should be initiated with sufficient authority behind it to carry it through successfully. Data collection should be on a continuing basis. Only through such a conscientious effort can the Army determine what it is really doing in rehabilitation, how this stacks up with other correctional programs, its successes and weaknesses, and how it may best be improved.

3] Regarding the correctional system as a whole, it is obvious that it is a "system" in the truest sense of the word. A change, or even improvement, in one aspect has repercussions on the various other goals and constraints throughout the program. No single goal can be sought to the exclusion of the rest, and overemphasis upon any one goal may be to the detriment of other necessary objectives.

Alterations must be coordinated with one another instead of being approached piecemeal. A conceptualization of the military correctional system in terms of "trade-offs," a term long familiar in material development, seems very appropriate. Under this conception (for example, in the development of an aircraft), as one aspect of the system is changed to achieve a higher level on one goal, the change may or may not lead to decline in the fulfillment of other goals. If not, the change is highly desirable; if so, it must be considered carefully. The optimal correctional system will be one which can best resolve the tensions between components and fulfill *all* of the goals to the greatest possible extent.

4

Interaction Patterns Among Military Prison Personnel

LEON D. HANKOFF

This study is directed toward an understanding of social relations in a penal institution. With the impact of delinquency on the American scene, a greater demand is being placed on the social sciences for answers. A critical area is that of the penal institution, society's time-honored method of handling the delinquents. Despite its shortcomings, the penal institution remains the necessary, if not the only, means of dealing with many delinquents. Any scientific utilization of existing penal facilities calls for an understanding beyond the conventional and material dimensions of the institution.

A dynamic understanding of the penal institution is not readily achieved. The psychiatrist entering a penal institution is impressed by the enormous barrier existing between himself and the prison population, both inmates and personnel. The penal institution exists for the restraint and punishment of offenders. Suspicion and secrecy are the order of the day. An unwritten but well-established prison code has set the prisoner against any confidential communication with authority (Miller, 1958). The custodial officers, on the other hand, are immersed in similar attitudes of vigilance. They have a nerve-racking job to do and their interest is centered about maximum security, discipline, and a convenient, autonomous daily routine (Powelson and Bendix, 1951). The psychiatrist, placing a high premium on individual needs and freedom of communication, finds his standards in marked contrast to the base line of penal regulations and attitudes. Powelson and Bendix considered this conflict of attitudes between the psychiatrist and the custodial officer and concluded that, for the present, there is no satisfactory professional solution for the psychiatrist who chooses to remain and work in the penal institution. They pointed up the corrosive influence of the prison environment on the psychiatrist's attitudes and his eventual conscious and unconscious surrender to authoritarianism. In addition to this conflict in his own values, the professional worker may encounter difficulty because of his appearance to custodial officers as a potential reformer or theoretician—the perennial conflict between the planner and executor of any operation. The custodial officer is intent on a well-oiled daily routine. He may be suspicious and disdainful of change, considering it as unproven, dangerous, or impractical. In discussing his experiences as an innovator on a prison psychiatric ward, Graff (1956) stated that the guards sometimes viewed the psychiatrist as "on the side of the inmates" against them. In this respect, it is of interest that wardens have found themselves relatively powerless when attempting to alter the basic attitudes or practices of their lower personnel echelons toward the prisoners. It would seem, then, that our successful intervention in the penal institution must begin with an understanding of the institutional ties of the individuals within it.

Much of the groundwork for understanding the penal environment has been done but the dynamics of the personnel remains largely uncharted. The emphasis in penal psychology has usually been on the inmate. As in the case of the mental hospital, investigation of the occupant has long preceded that of the custodian.

Clemmer (1940) provided the basis for an understanding of the prison environment in his comprehensive monograph but has reported few observations on the social field of the personnel. Clemmer described the prisoner's culture and its dynamics, demonstrating the stability of this culture despite population flux. Although acknowledging the stabilizing influence of the prisoner's code, Miller has pointed out its antirehabilitative and tyrannical effects, particularly when utilized by the custodial officers to maintain order. That a corollary personnel culture must exist side by side with this prisoner culture is apparent and has been alluded to in the fictional, if not the scientific, literature.

The present report is based on observations of five military penal institutions: three Marine Corps brigs, one Navy brig, and one Army stockade. It is felt that the institutions observed are representative of most military penal institutions, and that some of the information may be applied as well to problems of penal institutions generally.

One of the Marine Corps brigs will be used as the focus for the description, although observations from all five institutions contributed to the conclusions. As a military psychiatrist, the writer was able to make direct observation of the brig and collect information from the population over a one-year period. The military psychiatrist was called on for formal brig inspections, screening of personnel for brig duty, screening of prisoners for retention in service, and psychiatric treatment of personnel and prisoners. In addition, there were chance observations while transacting the formal brig matters, group discussions with personnel, and social contacts with brig officers. The discussion groups contained four to eight men having the same rank or brig function and were conducted in a nondirective manner, ostensibly concerned with prisoner management.

Observations

The formal trappings of the brig were that of a rigid military hierarchy, operating on a detailed daily schedule for both prisoners and personnel. The philosophy and functioning of the brig were stated meticulously in a brig manual, always on hand for policy decisions and instruction of incoming prisoners and personnel.

The physical plant of the brig is traditionally divided into two areas, the compound and the office. The compound is the prisoner's living area. In the particular brig under consideration, the compound was a large square enclosure, surrounded by a double barbed-wire fence, entered by a single gate, and punctuated at regular intervals by wooden frame watchtowers. The office was a small painted wooden building outside the compound near the gate. Here the administration of the brig was carried out, records kept, and orders issued.

The brig was operated by thirty-three officers and men. The

hierarchy was headed by two commissioned officers. Next in line to the officers was the staff, composed of four senior noncommissioned officers, one acting as warden and the other three as his assistants or alternates. The remaining twenty-seven men were designated as compound personnel and were divided into three types: *1*] turnkeys, who maintained the gate; *2*] tower sentries, who manned the watchtowers; and *3*] compound sentries, who maintained order within the compound. The hierarchy system was not only defined by rank and function but by physical sphere of activity as well. Thus, the officers and staff did their work largely in the office while the compound personnel had their posts at the gate, towers, or grounds of the compound, respectively. The turnkeys were the ranking enlisted men of the compound area, usually being junior noncommissioned officers. The prisoner population numbered fifty to sixty men.

Official communication was organized in typical chain of command or "line" fashion, that is, from the initiator to the next adjacent rank. Almost always a superior initiated the communication, and it was passed in orderly fashion along the line to successively lower ranks. Communication was rarely initiated by inferiors to superiors and even more rarely was there any direct communication between nonadjacent ranks, such as a commissioned officer and a compound sentry.

The commanding officer of the brig, a colonel, had many other duties along with his command of the brig. He had no office in the brig and his contacts with the brig were limited to brief formal inspections. His junior, designated the brig officer, had the actual executive function of the brig and spent most of his working day in the brig office. The contacts of the commissioned officers with brig personnel were extremely formal. The brig officer conducted all business matters through the brig warden and had little direct contact with any other enlisted men. When a commissioned officer entered the compound, the entire area was called to attention and usually remained rigidly so until he had completed his business. The brig officer learned about the brig activities through a set of daily reports and, unless he inquired, his picture of brig functioning was apt to be a rather lifeless one.

Much information did not reach him when situations could be handled comfortably by the staff. To avoid possible injustices, the device existed whereby any man in the brig—prisoner or personnel—might request a private meeting with the brig officer or submit an anonymous complaint. Generally, however, this system never achieved any great use or value among the lower echelons of the brig.

The four staff members may be regarded as "career men." All had considerable experience in the military penal institution and thoroughly understood its machinery. They were specialists in the execution of military penology. It was their assigned task to maintain overall order of the brig as well as of the lower-ranking enlisted men. The staff tended to regard the brig from the point of view of a conventional rule-book, which we may call the charter. In group discussions, staff members stated their mission in the brig very concretely, tended to minimize the brig's flaws, and attributed administrative problems to forces outside the brig such as inadequate funds, inadequate manpower, climatic and tactical factors.

The turnkeys occupied a somewhat intermediate position both in rank and function. They were junior noncommissioned officers, no longer involved in the laborious tasks of handling prisoners, but not sufficiently beyond the compound gate to occupy office staff positions. They generally presented an attitude of acceptance toward the brig organization, although they did not take as orthodox a view as the staff. In group discussions their thoughts often turned to matters of control and status in the brig. A recurring topic was the subject of "problem" prisoners. The turnkeys felt that the sentries were lax or cowardly in the handling of a surly prisoner. One prisoner in particular had roused their anger. This prisoner had maintained an apathetic, passively negativistic manner throughout his brig sentence; no measures or appeals could alter his uncooperative state. The turnkeys experienced intolerable feelings of impotence toward this man whom the brig could not break. Their feelings were somewhat assuaged by the thought that the brig manual severely limited their physical control over the prisoner. They often implied that some of the brig regulations concerning prisoner management were best ignored in dealing with such situations.

The actual handling of prisoners was carried out by the sentries, who represented the lowest-ranking, least-experienced, and youngest of the brig personnel. Their behavior toward superiors was usually one of impersonal military discipline and courtesy. Their management of prisoners was often embellished by personal expressions of hostility. Although no case of physical maltreatment at this brig had been proven, direct observation and multiple parallel accounts left no doubts that many sentries were quite uninhibited in the performance of acts of hostility toward prisoners. An entire armamentarium of methods of humiliation, provocation, and abuse was used by some, often with the feeling that this approach was the practical solution sanctioned by the authorities.

Group discussions with the sentries proved to be quite spirited and expressive. They felt strongly antagonistic toward the staff, particularly toward the warden. The sentries felt that the staff was their adversary, spying on them, judging them, and harassing them. The sentries protested that they were treated like prisoners and frequently compared their lot to that of their captives.

The sentries' hostility toward prisoners was presented to the interviewer in a rather indirect fashion in obvious deference to the interviewer's status, nor was this hostility associated with the group pride that characterized staff-directed hostility. Many of the sentries explained their hostility toward the prisoners as resulting from their own oppression by the staff. They said that they passed on to the prisoners the anger they experienced from the staff's harassment. After a personnel inspection by the warden, for example, one sentry found himself particularly hard on the prisoners because he had "no one else to take it out on." Furthermore, the prisoners were aware that the warden harassed the sentries and some sentries argued that their consequent loss of face made the prisoners harder to manage and necessitated firmer measures.

The group discussions with the sentries produced a surprising number of admissions of hostile acts against prisoners.

The incidents were usually presented in a modified or disguised manner. Personal accounts by the sentries were often presented with some demonstration of guilt or mock guilt. At times the "confession" concerned a very minor act that served as a screen for a more serious offense. Although the sentries were somewhat uncomfortable about their hostile acts toward prisoners, there was strong group feeling that stern physical measures are a desirable approach to prisoner control. The restrictions the brig manual imposed on the sentries were unanimously opposed by the group. At times righteous indignation ran high and the sentry saw himself as the dispenser of personalized true justice. One sentry cited an instance of a senior noncommissioned officer (NCO) who, as a prisoner, was allowed special privileges. The sentry resented these considerations to the wrongdoer. In this respect, it was noted that known homosexual prisoners are often particularly oppressed in the brig, freely insulted, and segregated. Only one sentry in the group took a stand against abuse of prisoners. He had been assigned to the brig just a few days previously. Others, who might have entered the brig environment with similar feelings, had already surrendered them to group pressure. Sympathy was quite unpopular.

Retaliation by the prisoners was a preoccupation of some sentries. Incidents were recalled where ex-prisoners had met former captors outside of the brig and exacted personal redress.

The sentries readily expressed criticism of other personnel groups. In addition to their open resentment of the staff's despotic authority the sentries were generally dissatisfied with their relationships with other personnel groups. They complained that there were exclusive "factions" in the brig personnel and that there was too much distinction between NCO and private. They stated that there should be more unity among the personnel, that the word of a sentry concerning prisoner "incidents" should be unquestioned, and that more action should be taken on sentries' complaints. They felt it was useless to approach the brig officer because they would either be intercepted by the warden or their gripes would be neutralized by his subsequent comments to the brig officer. The sentries also criticized subgroups within the sentry group. The compound sentries felt that the tower sentries and turnkeys tried to exert too much control over the prisoners from their peripheral positions and that this intervention was unnecessary and domineering. The sentries who were permanent brig personnel distinguished themselves from the sentries who had volunteered from other units for limited brig tours to fill out the brig complement and who they believed were poorly motivated and did an inferior job.

In discussions with the sentries, the phenomenon of the group leader was regularly observed. The sentries were seen in groups of five or six; and one or two usually functioned as the spokesmen for each group. These few were assertive and outspoken, often resorted to profanity, and were most open in their criticism of authority. They tended to set the themes of discussion for the group and used introductory key words or incidents to invite group participation on the target subject. These same men were also the most outspoken in their expressions of hostility toward prisoners and their wishes for physical punishment of prisoners. In the group interviews, the spokesmen were sometimes paired. They usually supported each other and passed mutual opinions back and forth across the group.

Although the focus of the observations is on brig personnel, it is obvious that personnel relationships did not function in a vacuum apart from the prisoners. Prisoner activities did affect personnel relations, and the usual stimulus was some form of prisoner misconduct. In terms of actual brig observations, the misconduct had a kind of periodicity. As it built up, the brig officer would become aware of a constant series of incidents with prisoners being put on report by the sentries. The prisoners would engage in smuggling and horseplay, feign illness or exhaustion, and fight among themselves. Various counteractions would be taken by the personnel.

In dealing with prisoner misconduct, mass punishment was often resorted to, that is, all the prisoners were punished for the fault of one recalcitrant or undetected prisoner. Prisoners' cliques would be broken up by segregation or by rearrangement of sleeping quarters. With continued measures, prisoner misconduct would suddenly or gradually taper off, and average conditions would prevail until the next pitch built up.

Interaction Patterns

In attempting to formulate patterns of brig personnel behavior, it is of value to use varying frames of reference, approaching the situation in terms of both group and individual psychology. An effort has been made to delineate the approaches, but contaminations are inevitable.

From the standpoint of group relations, our chief interest is in the informal elements that have grown out of the military ingredients forming the brig. This informal structure or internal system, to use Homans' term (1950), appears to be an extension of the existing rank structure, in which each subgroup is socially isolated and suspicious of the others. The enlisted personnel of the brig grouped themselves rigidly into three echelons based on their formal functions and ranks: the staff, the turnkeys, and the compound and tower sentries. These lines of division were evident during on-duty fraternization as well as during off-duty recreation. Changes in personnel did not affect the fundamental patterns, for incoming personnel achieved the set standards within a short period after their arrival. Nor did the youthfulness of many of the sentries give them any greater flexibility or mobility in their roles. All echelons will be discussed; but the main consideration will be given to the lowest level, the sentries, who constituted seventeen of the thirty-three brig personnel and who fell heir to the most discontent and conflict.

Several features of the overall brig group may be discerned. The first is the nature of communication or interaction. Communication was almost always initiated from above, almost always had a negative or authoritarian quality, and almost never allowed for redress or interaction with its initiator. Other fairly generalized features were: the conflict between classes and with authority, hostility chain reactions, and rationalized substitute acting-out in a downward direction.

Beginning with the two officers, we see a picture of almost complete detachment. Orders are given, reports received, and unless something very unusual occurs the officers remain quite uninvolved with the human aspects of their personnel. Of any brig personnel, they most closely approximate their formal role. It is likely that they would have acted on information concerning undesirable brig practices but this knowledge seldom reached them.

The staff, while not uninvolved in the brig social relations, showed a similar picture of security and clear-cut aims. They exerted much authority over the men below them and rarely received an order from their superiors that was not passed on to men below them. They tended to be somewhat disdainful of the officers, secretly believing themselves to be the significant operating personnel, better off if unhindered by the officers' impractical and academic ideas.

The turnkeys are bypassed by much of the one-way communication of the brig. They have been promoted out of the sentry position to the gate and aspire to the next higher stage in the office. Thus concerned with status, they are critical of the sentries and concerned about the undominated prisoner. In terms of individual psychology, it may be said that the turnkey's preoccupation with the problem prisoner is a projection of his own feeling of lack of dominance within the personnel hierarchy.

The brig structure appears to weigh most heavily on the sentry. He is at the bottom of the one-way chain of orders. He is unable to reciprocate with the initiator, receives little in the way of supportive or positive interaction from superiors, and is often left in doubt concerning his acceptance by superiors. The conscious hostility for the staff, aired in group discussions, appears to be a natural outgrowth of the frustrating situation. Even if the sentry wanted to demonstrate positive sentiment for his superiors, he has no access to them. Concurrent with the hostile sentiment toward the staff is the hostile activity toward the prisoners. Prisoner abuse may perhaps serve a "homeostatic" function for the beleaguered sentries, in terms of their group position. It serves to emphasize the sentry's position in the personnel ranks and provides him with a partial mastery of his environment.

Certain sentiments within the brig atmosphere facilitated the hostile behavior of sentries toward prisoners: r] A moralistic attitude prevailed among the personnel that "the prisoners are here to learn a lesson." 2] The sentry group did not attach any stigma to acts of prisoner abuse. 3] The sentries thought that their insignificance in the personnel rank encouraged the prisoners to be insolent and made harsh measures a necessity. 4] The sentries thought that they were unsupported by their superiors in cases of prisoner misconduct and that they themselves had to settle the score with the prisoner at his own level.

Discussion

The sadistic practices of the sentries upon the prisoners appear to be plausibly explained by the factors of group equilibrium and group sanctions. However, the process whereby the individual perceives an insult, responds with hostile feelings, and achieves satisfaction through a hapless third party has really not been adequately explained. The fractioning of the sentry's negative sentiment has been described in terms of group behavior but is not explained by the present observations.

A similar problem has been considered by Thorne (1957), who charted the "epidemiology of hostility" through family studies. Thorne has pointed out the contagious quality of hostility, its tendency toward chain reactions, and its extreme potency when the recipient is in an inescapable position. The application of his thesis to institutions is apparent and appears borne out by the present observations of a penal institution. The sentries, our youngest siblings of the brig family, feel subject to inescapable frustration and hostility. The sentry is often young, inexperienced, lacks mature outlets, and is hard pressed to deal with his "chronic anger state." Standards within his peer group sanction downward acting-out, and he readily translates pressures from his superiors as well as neurotic hostility into aggression toward the prisoners. Of course, the cycle does not end there. Although severely restricted, the prisoners retaliate with negativism, accidents, sluggishness, and malingering. A further result, pointed out by Thorne, is the buildup of mutually suspicious and paranoid attitudes (Thorne, 1953). Although not striking in the present study, marked paranoid attitudes on the part of prison personnel have been described in other studies (Jacobson, 1949). Thorne's epidemiologic framework is a useful approach to the subject. An interesting sidelight on the epidemiology of hostility is the practice of mass punishment in the brig. Implicit in this device is the wish that the group will become enraged and turn on the one, enforcing the discipline of the authority. Thus, mass punishment is the planned use of the retaliation motif to maintain control.

Another of the phenomena to be considered in the shaping of the sentry group sentiments and activities is that of the group leader. As noted, there were among the sentries certain individuals who were quite outspoken and who took the lead in criticism of the staff and discussions of prisoner abuse. This syndrome of assertive group behavior, hostility for prisoners, and hostility for authority may be viewed in various contexts: *1] The individual.* The spokesman may be the more basically hostile and aggressive member of the personnel group and maintain this position in the relationships observed: toward the interview, toward the prisoner, and toward the superior. *2] The sentry group.* Hostile impulses and acts have produced inner conflict and the individual seeks resolution of his discomfort through the available communication medium, the group meeting. The man who feels guilty or otherwise uneasy about his hostile acts may seek to express himself, to talk away his discomfort in a receptive atmosphere. He seeks to gain group acceptance and line group support for his own dubious standards. *3] The brig culture.* The aggressive sentries have become the reflectors of the hostile retaliatory elements in the penal atmosphere. Hostile reactions to the staff and prisoners and his personal life fuse in his mind into a hopeless jumble of anger. Furthermore, anger and rage are more condoned as a masculine form of expression than are more "feminine" feelings of sympathy or depression.

In considering intrapsychic or personality factors, one is faced with the immediate pitfall of generalizing from group observation to individual functioning. As a group, the sentries were characterized by authority conflict, a high level of hostility, and acting-out in substituted or available situations. Although it cannot be assumed that this corresponds to the personality of the average sentry, it is probable that these are features of many sentries that become aggravated in the brig setting. In terms of group personality, it is of interest to compare the orderly brig personnel organization with present-day delinquency culture. The conflict with authority, the reservoir of hostility, and the ready acting-out, all seen in brig personnel interaction patterns, are quite discernible in modern delinquency patterns. The headline-making modern young delinquent is often marked by his viciousness, vandalism, and flouting of the law. Within this particular brig, 133 successive prisoners who were delinquents were evaluated psychiatrically. The majority of these showed features of chronic anger and authority conflict within the substrate of a character disorder. Are prisoner and sentry struggling with the same basic problems? The growing delinquency problems and trends of Western culture suggest that authority conflict is a universal theme. Our present-day culture is marked by rejection of the elder, disdain for education, and cult of youth, all pointing to the conflict with established order (Linden, 1957). The brig prisoner is the unsuccessful protestant, the sentry the successful one sensitized to despotic authority.

Sentries often gave evidence of their identification with prisoners in the group discussions, comparing themselves to prisoners in light of the staff's activities toward them. A frequent expression was that the sentry would end up a prisoner if goaded too far.

Guilty fear was evidenced by the sentry's preoccupation with prisoner retaliation. The sentry may be staving off his prison identification through his sadistic rejection of the prisoner. In a study of prison guards, Jacobson has pointed out that the guard's reaction to this identification may serve to aggravate his severity toward the prisoners. In this same light it may be seen that criticism or rejection by superiors is quite threatening to the sentry because it tends to separate him from the personnel and push him more toward identification with the prisoner. Another factor to be considered in the sentry's developing sentiments is that of his proximity to the prisoners. The sentry is almost certain to have more human feelings for a prisoner whom he guards all day than for an officer whom he salutes once a week. The sentry is thus in a position to acquire the attitudes of the prisoner directly and this may well contribute to their similarity.

Summary and Conclusions

Observations were made on five military penal institutions: three Marine Corps brigs, one Navy brig, and one Army stockade. The interaction patterns of the personnel of one of the Marine Corps brigs, representative of the several institutions studied, are described. The thirty-three men in the brig formed a rigid hierarchy characterized by overt discipline and covert hostility. Hostile forces reinforced each other, and a reverberating cycle was maintained in the brig through all levels.

Sadism engendered in brig personnel was similar to processes operating in many inmates. The potent atmosphere of the penal institution is anti-rehabilitative, prevents improvement by piecemeal measures, and might be the minimal focus of professional intervention.

Professional intervention in penal functioning has often had disappointing results. From the data presented it may be understood why piecemeal measures are unsuccessful in prisons. The tyranny of roles in the populace overrules most material changes. Usually little effort is made to change institutions on an attitudinal level. At this state of knowledge, when material needs of humane standards can generally be met, it seems reasonable to assume that the crucial area to attack is that of the attitudes of the milieu. Furthermore, the attitudes of the lowest level of functionary appear deserving of the most attention. In the penal institution here observed, if one is forced to choose between the psychiatric care and guidance of personnel and that of the prisoners, attention given to personnel would appear to be most rewarding in its overall rehabilitative effect on the prisoners.

5

A Technic
for Military Delinquency Management

BRUCE BUSHARD *and*
ARNOLD W. DAHLGREN

The study reported here is based upon a two-and-one-half-year experience during which the Mental Hygiene Consultation Service (MHCS) became a continuous, cooperating, assisting agency in a stockade operation. It provides a history of the development of this technic and proposes a *modus operandi*. During the period of this operation, the recidivism rate has fallen, the number of disturbances has diminished, and the management of the psychiatric workload has become an easily handled flow rather than a spotty, difficult problem accented by many emergencies. In addition to improvement in those areas which lend themselves to statistical study, there has been an increased conviction on the part of all persons who participate that "at least something is being done."

The Stockade and Stockade Prisoners

The stockade itself is not usually a central concern of a military commander. Especially on a basic-training post, it is a sort of "backwater," for the commander is aware that the military potential of the inmates is generally low. His time and energy are directed primarily at the training on nondelinquent individuals who present a good many problems themselves.

Persons who are confined no longer participate in basic training and are, for this reason, transferred out of their basic unit into a "replacement company." This company is also the official unit of apprehended individuals from other Army areas, deserters, and any other person who for any reason—frequently

nondelinquent—does not participate in training. The delinquent thus ceases to be a part of an organization in which he is
known. His former commander has neither responsibility for
nor interest in him. The commander of the replacement company does not even see him. He is of interest to and is known by
the confinement officer and his staff alone. For MHCS purposes
the group might be defined as a screened collection of individuals of poor military adaptation potential.

In view of these factors, the stockade at Ft. Dix, New Jersey
was, in 1954, a serious problem area. The prisoners were sullen
and uncooperative, the population was large, running at about
18 per thousand troops, and the number in disciplinary segregation was high, being at times 10.4 per hundred prisoners. Prisoners with two or more convictions accounted for 30 percent of
the population, and the number of persons with three or more
convictions was substantial. Finally, individual and organized
rebellion was a frequent occurrence, requiring the attention
of the post commander.

This culminated, in the fall of 1954, in a major disturbance
in the course of which nearly all order was lost and the custodial
personnel were driven from a section of the stockade. Even an
effort by the commanding general himself to quell the riot was
unsuccessful and he was nearly injured when rocks were thrown
at him.

When order was restored and the guard complement aug-
mented, an overall reorganization of the system of handling
delinquents was directed. Certain of the custodial personnel
were replaced and a more understanding yet firmer attitude was
initiated and maintained.

Investigators were appointed to screen the population and
to recommend action to be taken in individual cases. These
officers found problems abounding in the population. There
were persons who had as many as seven prior convictions. Some
had literally never served an honorable day, and there were
many more whose total honorable service fell to 10 percent of
their total service. There was no established way to expedite the
elimination of narcotic addicts, alcoholics, or homosexuals
whose very presence serves as a nidus for disruption, temptation, and disorder in any prison. Although the mass of the sen-

tenced prisoners were in confinement for minor offenses, many of them were so antisocial that a prison of less than maximum security represented more nearly a challenge for escape attempts than a reliable means of retention. Not only were they a direct source of disciplinary problems, but they were uncommonly capable of leading others astray and organizing concerted efforts at resistance to authority.

The nature of military justice is such that persons entering confinement are rarely true first offenders. Examination of the history of an individual confinee will ordinarily reveal that his earliest offenses, if purely military, were first overlooked. Later ones were dealt with through Article 15, Uniform Code of Military Justice, a nonjudicial punishment administered by the commanding officer. His first sentence to confinement is usually suspended. In the main, the confinee has been offered both extensive counseling by various agencies and a good deal of "easy" or "gentle" disciplining. Simple advice or forgiveness has been proven to have insufficient impact to lead to improved behavior.

From the prisoner's point of view, the situation is hopeless. He either consciously rejects his military obligation or, if he accepts it, has found some reason for not fulfilling it. He expresses the opinion that he must take care of his mother, or his wife, or the family business, or he has some other excuse. In erecting such a rationalization, he finds both an excuse for his misbehavior and a basis for anger at the Army because it does not take the necessary action to return him to his home. Angry when first confined he is then most resistant to any type of rehabilitative effort.

From the commander's point of view, the problem is also great. Here is a man who, despite frequent offers of special consideration, continues to behave in an angry, inflammatory, and insubordinate manner. The commander, therefore, is forced to assume that if he continues to tolerate this behavior others will follow suit. The officer who has contact with such an individual almost certainly becomes angry, and often allows his attitude to become one in which desire to "show this guy a thing or two" becomes a factor.

Thus, by the time a soldier has been confined, both he and

the individuals dealing with him have sometimes lost their perspective so completely that the situation is at an impasse. The prisoner behaves in a manner which serves him poorly and the individuals who deal with him have allowed their emotions to control the situation to the degree that they accomplish little save to give the prisoner a good excuse for his anger.

The outcome of this situation varies, but there is a common and readily observable pattern, primarily based upon the simple fact that the prisoner's anger usually causes trouble to no one but himself. Unless he is able to organize with others in such a way as to bring discomfort to the organization through his anger, he simply compounds his situation.

At a period that ranges ordinarily between the thirtieth and sixtieth day, the average prisoner is least recalcitrant. The difference between his attitude at that point and his attitude when he was first confined may be dramatic. If an observer is sensitive, he will note some effort on the part of the prisoner to achieve some type of nondelinquent acceptance. He sometimes must do this covertly lest he suffer rejection by his fellow prisoners if it becomes evident to them. Nevertheless, he frequently makes some effort in this direction. This might be interpreted as the point at which authority has won the struggle. When this occurs, the prisoner is ready to comply and sometimes merely seeks some way to return to the good graces of authority in a reasonably dignified manner. If, during this period, opportunities are available for parole, clemency, or other procedures in which a degree of acceptance or at least partial trust and forgiveness are implicit, he may be moved away from his identification with delinquency and toward a more meaningful relationship with society. If such procedures are not available, he will ordinarily lapse into a type of apathy, retain or intensify his relation with the delinquent group, and become a poor risk for rehabilitation or a severe delinquency problem within the stockade itself.

This process may then be described as one in which the prisoner has two models with which to relate and to identify. He may identify with the prisoner group and indulge in the misapprehension that delinquency is a pattern of behavior with social value. On the other hand, he may identify with the custodial group who represent "society" and attempt to emulate their more successful transactions with their environment. Although the first identification is usually with the prisoner group, many prisoners will shift their identifications from one extreme to the other in the manner described. Rehabilitation is derived, then, partly from timing the offering of clemency at the moments when the more acceptable identification is in the ascendancy.

This program is designed to promote group forces which tend to press individuals toward nondelinquent patterns of behavior. This is accomplished through providing the prisoner group with only that information on which they can predict what will occur if they conform with normal social attitudes and behavior patterns.

They must know that if they conform in a proper manner, opportunities exist for eventual restoration to a satisfactory position in society. They must not be able to predict what frightening or threatening statements they can make to secure an early release, special attention, or disorganization of the administration. They will soon sense the existence of a too rigid policy which, for example, requires that all individuals given to a certain act be discharged from the service immediately. They will then have information available as to the price they must pay to get out of the stockade or the Army. To deal with each such case on its own merits tends to produce a sufficiently varied pattern of administrative response so that such an outcome can be avoided and the prisoner group can be deprived of knowledge of such policies even if they exist.

The Program

The reorganization of the stockade operation was accomplished through the establishment of three routines:

1] A post level agency was delegated the responsibility to consider discharge from the service for all individuals following their third conviction by court-martial. Processing takes place in such a way that completion of sentence and discharge from the service, if approved, are coincident. This averts the problem that many of these people will not remain on the post long enough to be discharged after release from confinement.

2] The confinement officer was to institute rehabilitative programs:

a] All employable prisoners were to be given work with which they were familiar or were to learn new, employable skills of value to the military. Their use in pointless menial labor was to be avoided. Shops were started for their employment in painting signs, repairing targets and tentage, and other menial but not degrading work.

b] Mature attitudes were to be maintained. Military discipline was to be used in its constructive sense toward rehabilitation and not in a merely punitive manner, for "brutality and lax discipline go hand in hand."

c] A rehabilitation company was established. This was a minimum security portion of the stockade located outside of the prison walls with prisoners in parolee status. A board consisting of the commanding officer of the prisoner battalion, the stockade chaplain, and a member of MHCS was appointed and designated by the Classification Board. Any sentenced prisoner was eligible for assignment to this company upon the recommendation of the board and upon the approval of the confinement officer. The decision was based upon the prisoner's behavior and his apparent rehabilitative potential. While in the rehabilitation company, the prisoner completed his training by being attached, during appropriate hours, to a unit in the proper phase of training. If he was not a trainee, he became available for other work.

d] The clemency system was enhanced by appointing a board of officers as a Clemency Board. This board may recommend suspension of sentence after the prisoner has served between one-third and one-half of his sentence. This recommendation is dependent upon his behavior, attitude, and rehabilitative potential.

e] The system of parole was enhanced. Prisoners who could be employed about the post were placed on parolee status when it was reasonable, in the judgment of the confinement officer, to do so and they were allowed to go from their place of employment without a guard.

3] The Mental Hygiene Consultation Service enhanced and formalized its relationship to the stockade. The MHCS had, from its inception, some type of relationship to the stockade. At times various programs were established for short periods, but these rarely included the total prisoner population and never represented a real, cooperative, combined effort with both command and psychiatric personnel participating. The following procedures were adopted:

a] All prisoners were examined within fourteen days after the pronouncing of sentence. Pretrial examinations were prompt if and when requested by the commander or the defense or trial counsels.

b] Persons requiring psychotherapy received it.

c] Persons, especially first offenders, likely to benefit from transfer to the rehabilitation company or clemency were referred to the Classification Board or the Clemency Board at the appropriate times.

d] Close liaison was maintained with the confinement officer in finding mutually agreed to solutions for such problems as tantrums, suicidal gestures, suspected psychosis, evidence of organized resistance, cliques, etc.

e] When rehabilitative efforts were attempted and significant evidence of their lack of success amassed, positive recommendations for separation from the service were made.

The MHCS remained conservative in recommending separation for persons with fewer than three convictions on record. It was regarded as unlikely that such persons, whatever their verbal attitudes, would be offered the full effort of rehabilitation. Any person, whatever his number of courts-martial, in whose case there was reasonable evidence of homosexuality, alcoholism, drug addiction, or antisocial tendencies beyond the capacity of the stockade to control, was recommended for separation. Remission of sentence in order to expedite discharge was also recommended.

The procedures were so constructed that command was assured that no individual would in effect get "lost" and simply stay on indefinitely, neither being disposed of definitively nor rendering meaningful service. It can be seen that MHCS occupied a central position, as the initiating agency in much of this program.

THE ROLE OF THE STOCKADE PERSONNEL

The custodial personnel must exercise mature judgment and practice penology at its highest level. They must attempt to suppress their tendency to become angry with the prisoners. They must be mature enough to avert the repeated efforts of persons who, for lack of understanding, wish to "put some real punishment into that place." Efforts to secure the labor of prisoners to clear the streets, to rake leaves, or to do more than their fair share of the post's menial tasks must be critically examined. The confinement officer must be aware of and prepared to defend the bases for denying such efforts at any time the major and overriding aims of the programs might thus be sacrificed.

The confinement officer must recognize that essential to his behavior is the championing of the nondelinquent patterns of the prisoner. He is not only the prisoner's custodian, he is also his spokesman. To the degree that he can, the confinement officer must protect his charges from loss of dignity and individuality while demanding discipline. He will get the latter if he gives the former. Prisoners will tell one, for example, that they are at their most undignified and at their angriest when walking about the post under guard. Securing authorization for a bus to transport them may lead to a great deal more rehabilitation than hours of lecture or pious "understanding."

Finally, the stockade officer must enter into a cooperative relationship with the psychiatrist. When a problem that appears to have psychiatric implications arises, it is essential that the confinement officer and the psychiatrist develop a mutually acceptable procedure, and the confinement officer carry out his portion willingly. If it is decided that a given suicidal gesture, for example, would be best handled by ignoring it, he must be willing to do so. Although the psychiatrist functions only as his advisor, the confinement officer must recognize that psychiatric findings and recommendations are technical suggestions that are perhaps best judged by a trial.

THE ROLE OF THE MENTAL HYGIENE CONSULTATION SERVICE

This service must recognize that a substantial amount of its responsibility lies within the stockade. It must accept the presuppositions upon which stockades are operated and attempt to accomplish its end within that framework. Doing the actual work within the stockade is not only easier and more economical administratively, but it places the Mental Hygiene Consultation Service staff in the position of an insider in immediate and operating contact with stockade problems rather than remaining an esoteric, overcritical outside agency.

The Mental Hygiene Consultation Service staff must recognize that a prison is a place in which society imposes control upon persons who will not or cannot control themselves. Regardless of psychiatric opinions, a degree of punishment continues to be a part of the system. This leads to anxiety, depression, rebelliousness, and recalcitrance among many of the prisoners, and these are the natural consequences of imprisonment. The psychiatrist can rarely do much about it except to exert himself toward helping the prisoner avoid future repetition. He must also recognize that early experiences in a stockade are certain to give rise to adaptational anxiety which will, in time, be resolved. He must be aware of the normal cause of such anxiety in order to know what to expect, lest his overconcern lead him to imply that he can do more to manipulate the prisoner's situation than lies within his purview.

The psychiatrist must cooperate with and respect the custodial staff. His visits to the stockade must be at frequent enough intervals so that the normal prisoner can be handled in a routine manner.

A smoothly functioning routine is an essential to this program. It may, more effectively than any other influence, make it evident that this anxiety, that reality need, or this depression are expectable and ponderable. The prisoner who appears without an appointment, the prisoner referred by the dispensary physician, the prisoner who makes a request to see a particular person at MHCS are all suspect. In the main, such a person is seeking a special handling one cannot really give him. These individuals should be turned away and required to follow the usual procedure. This is, of course, possible only if they were seen in the normal course of events.

In practical fact, the mass of the work done in the program was done by social workers. They interviewed all new prisoners after trial and made an effort to interpret the prisoner's behavior to him. Reality problems such as concern for family, allotments, and other such matters were also covered. The most important function of the interview, however, was to lay the groundwork for the remainder of the program. This interchange between prisoner and social worker provided an experience, in which acceptance is offered as an opportunity for coming to terms with the administration. The prisoner was shown that lack of social conformity has been of little value to him. The essence was that such antisocial attitudes are, in this interview as they are in other contacts with the administration, simply not the basis on which transactions are allowed to take place.

The social worker also sat as a member of both the Classification Board and the Clemency Board. Beyond this, the MHCS staff performed only those services at the stockade that are requested, attempting not to interfere with its routine.

Although the stark and unhappy stories told to the social worker are frequently fabrications, care was taken to make certain that the individuals doing this work did not become cynical. Any reasonably believable story was checked by requesting a home-conditions report from the American Red Cross. Such information was not only of value to the psychiatric staff, but also helpful to the commander in arriving at administrative decisions.

Finally, the MHCS must recognize that although much that goes on partakes of psychiatric considerations, it by no means follows that the MHCS always has a contribution to make, to say nothing of a solution to offer. When this became evident, such contributions as may be appropriate were made, and the staff carefully withdrew from the situation.

PROCEDURES

Twice weekly, the confinement officer prepared a list of the newly sentenced prisoners in the stockade. This was forwarded to the MHCS through the appropriate personnel section which add essential data such as the number of courts-martial, the commander's opinion, etc. A social-work officer had two periods of consultation a week at the stockade during which he saw every person so listed. He investigated the background of the case, discussed it with the commanding officers where indicated, and made a report to the stockade commander. Individuals referred to the psychiatrist were seen routinely the following week during one or two regularly scheduled periods with the confinement officer and the decisions made. During these periods, the psychiatrist also examined any person or group referred by custodial personnel, did pretrial sanity determinations on the request of the Judge Advocate General and saw persons referred by the other sources.

In situations in which the recommendation was for clemency, transfer to the rehabilitation company, or special work assignments and limitations, or when it was upon other matters that constitute recommendations to the confinement officer, the final report was provided to the confinement officer and was used by the various boards. The confinement officer and the psychiatrist work together particularly closely in arriving at technics for handling cases of individual pathology or of failure to adapt to the confinement situation.

In cases where elimination from the service was recommended, the report was provided to the newly founded agency where it was heard immediately if such was the recommendation, or it was placed in a suspense file to be heard at such a time as to assure that the individual will not return to an active-duty status.

Evaluation of the Program

The success of prison operation ordinarily depends upon the degree of discipline and cooperation the custodial personnel are capable of maintaining. The premise is that the degree of area restraint necessary and the rate at which the disciplinary action is necessary are direct measures of poor discipline and restiveness in the population.

Before the program was inaugurated, nearly 20 percent of the prisoners were in maximum custody and fewer than 10 percent were on parolee status. About 70 percent were in medium or maximum custody, seemingly indicating marked dependence upon area restraint. After the program was put into operation, maximum custody fell as low as 5 percent and never rose above about 10 percent. Maximum plus medium custody accounted for 50 percent or less of the population during most of the reported period. Parolee status was awarded to from 20 to 25 percent of the population, while during most of the period minimum custody plus parole accounted for about one-half of the population. In general, the data seem to indicate a substantial diminution in the use of area restraint.

The question arises as to whether this easing of restraint led to an increase in restiveness. Sick call represents one traditional way of expressing dissatisfaction. The sick-call rate at a post stockade is usually considerably greater than in the post at large. After starting with a rate more than seven times that of the post, the stockade showed a general diminution to less than five times the general rate.

Such restiveness and resistance to the general discipline of the stockade might be expected to manifest itself in an increased number of disciplinary actions within the stockade itself. There was a marked diminution in the use of both disciplinary segregation and court-martial. The annual rate of disciplinary segregation per thousand stockade population dropped from 1756 to under 400. The courts-martial rate dropped from 450 to 150 per annum. These measures have been regarded by the custodial personnel as much less necessary.

When the Rehabilitation Company was first established, nearly all of its members promptly went AWOL (absent without leave). This was blamed upon faulty screening technics, but whatever the reason, the AWOL rate of this group (the mass of whom are confined because of AWOL) has, since that time, been generally lower than that of the post at large. A three-day home parole has been given both Christmases and only one prisoner has violated it. A program like this requires, then, one undeniable consideration: The command must be interested enough to tolerate some early growing pains and must recognize that such incidents are only outstanding examples of the renowned tendency of prisoners to test the limits—to see how far they can go. Everyone must be willing to take a chance and to recognize that some problem will arise. To operate the stockade in such a way as to avoid problems decreases opportunities for rehabilitation.

The incidence of escape from the stockade proper has remained relatively constant in spite of the diminution of "custody grade consciousness." The rate approximates or is lower than the post AWOL rate. The small size of the rehabilitation company is such that one elopement produces a gigantic value when expressed as a rate per thousand per annum. Since the early incident of almost total elopement, as long as nine months has elapsed without an escape, and during the remaining period one or two prisoners have been the maximum to escape during any three-month period.

Within the stockade there was a disappearance of recidivism beyond five times and a near disappearance of recidivism beyond four times. Approximately 18 percent of the population had had three or more previous courts-martial prior to the onset of the program. This figure dropped to approximately 5 percent. The incidence of first offenders did not change significantly.

The number of confined individuals per thousand means that post population was greater in this stockade than is typical of posts army-wide. To some degree at least, this reflects the presence of a substantial number of individuals from other posts apprehended in local areas and confined at Ft. Dix for disposition. The program described has, however, been accompanied by a gradual diminution in the number of prisoners per thousand mean post population, which now approaches more nearly the average post's experience. The incidence dropped from a high of 18 prisoners per thousand troops to about 10 prisoners per thousand troops. The establishment of an overseas replacement station in the middle of this period produced no appreciable change in the data.

Psychiatric results have been even more difficult to evaluate. The incidence of referrals to MHCS from the stockade, expressed as the rate per thousand per annum, before and after initiation of this coordinated program about doubled. It is believed, however, that the amount of time and effort expended on referrals from the stockade has remained about the same.

Such a coordinated program makes it easier to achieve results because more can be done for more people at less expense in time and effort. The types of cases encountered show only the expectable preponderance of antisocial types of character disorder. The incidence of psychosis and of other psychologically determined symptoms is not significantly different than the incidence elsewhere on the post. Transfers to the rehabilitation company have never been made in large numbers. The census of that operation has remained more or less constant at about one-tenth of the total population.

A study has been conducted of the results of the rehabilitation program as measured by the reported opinions of the commanding officers of the units to which "graduates" of the program are assigned. The reports made by these officers in response to a letter sent to them ninety days after restoration indicated that 58 percent of the restorees were successful, with a total of 45 percent receiving "good" or "excellent" evaluations. Of the remaining 42 percent, 27 percent were returned to a stockade, 12 percent went AWOL, and 3 percent received undesirable discharges. Thirty percent of the commanding officers did not respond. In considering these results we should note that criteria of efficacy in any rehabilitative procedure are difficult to establish. In the case of the rehabilitation of delinquents, the problem is made to appear even more bleak by the modesty of results under the best of circumstances.

It is impossible to establish which of these effects can be ascribed to the psychiatric program per se. A tendency exists to overevaluate the psychiatric contributions and to underrate the value of custodial staff attitudes, the availability of work programs, and staff and command cooperation. There is probably an even more significant tendency to fail to recognize the importance of cooperation and mutual respect among these agencies. Although the custodial personnel may benefit from having access to psychiatric understanding of abnormal behavior, the psychiatrist has much to learn about normal prisoner behavior from the custodial personnel. The psychiatric influence would be of value in the situation even if it only amounted to the nonspecific fact that the post commander is able to look upon psychiatric opinion as being relatively dispassionate, and the custodial personnel are able to proceed in their own ways at times as a result of psychiatric reassurance that a given prisoner is not psychotic.

Summary

The pressures presently impinging upon the commander of a post in the U.S. Army are such that a stockade must be operated in a fashion that will avoid incidents leading to danger to life or limb. In addition, the prisoner group contains a high percentage of persons of low military potential whose disposition is economically advantageous once the degree of potential has been clearly established. A program of mutual cooperation between stockade and psychiatric personnel appears to be an effective device to attain this end. A constructive program for the rehabilitation of those who can be reclaimed is described. This program appears to avert the confirmation of delinquent behavior as a persistent behavior pattern which leads to an unnecessarily high loss of personnel.

6

Multidisciplinary Approach to Prisoner Rehabilitation in the Air Force

GEORGE J. BRODER

Shortly after the reorganization of the United States military services in 1947, the newly-created Department of the Air Force initiated a review of its personnel policies. The then Air Provost Marshal was assigned the responsibility for recommending changes in the methods of handling Air Force prisoners. The impetus for seeking these changes was the growing belief that a large percentage of these offenders were not criminals in the ordinary sense, and, that with appropriate methods of rehabilitation, many of these young men could contribute significantly to the Air Force.

Subsequent study and consideration of the problem culminated in September 1951 when a "Plan for the Establishment and Operation of the Air Force Retraining Center" was approved. The Air Force was now ready to begin its program in prisoner rehabilitation. On 5 February 1952, a thirty-seven-year-old airman arrived at the 3320th Retraining Group, Amarillo AFB, Texas, and became Retrainee No. 1. Since thus becoming operational, the Retraining Group has now received almost eight thousand Air Force prisoners representing all major air commands, and whose offenses cover almost the entire spectrum of antisocial behavior.

Throughout these years, the primary mission of the Retraining Group has remained the same: *to return the maximum number of airmen to useful active duty with the Air Force.* To achieve this mission the Retraining Group has utilized the principle of a *multidisciplinary* approach to prisoner rehabilitation within the framework of a *Therapeutic Community.*

This paper will attempt to describe that community and how it operates to achieve its mission.

Treatment versus Punishment

The 3320th Retraining Group is a major confinement facility of the United States Air Force. Its mission and operation are unique, and no other similar program exists in the Air Force or in any other military service throughout the world. The program of the Retraining Group is designed to study the individual Retrainee and to provide a course of rehabilitation that will restore him to duty improved in attitude, conduct, and military efficiency, and able to perform useful service to the Air Force.

The emphasis of the Retraining Group is thus on correctional rehabilitation and not on institutional confinement. As such, the approach is one of treatment, rather than the traditional punishment of military offenders. To accomplish its mission, the Retraining Group utilizes many of the most advanced organizational and operational concepts developed by the behavioral sciences.

The Retraining Group operates under the overall responsibility of the Office of Security and Law Enforcement of the Air Training Command. Amarillo AFB has been one of the five major technical training centers of the Air Force. Such a training center provides numerous and diversified job outlets found only at larger bases, and selected Retrainees can be placed in the formal technical-school courses offered there.

The Retraining Group occupies an eight-acre tract of land on one portion of Amarillo AFB. To the casual observer, the Group cannot be distinguished in its general appearance from other units on the Base. The Retrainee arriving at the Group finds that he will live in a normal Air Force environment, although he is officially in confinement.

Only those rules and regulations necessary to provide a minimum degree of custody are permitted. There are no fences, guards, bars, or weapons; nor are individual room doors locked at night. Discipline is similar to that of a normal Air Force organization. Minor infractions are handled through counseling activities. Major infractions are reviewed by a disciplinary Adjustment Board, and are considered in relation to the Retrainee's overall progress in the Group.

The Retrainee has relative freedom to come and go within the Retraining Group area. As he advances in the program, the Retrainee is allowed to attend most Base facilities and some specified off-Base activities. Married men may stay with their wives in the Base Guest House if their wives or families visit the Group.

The Retrainees

The Retraining Group is currently programmed to handle 180 Air Force prisoners at any one time. Approximately 500 airmen, representing about 10 percent of all Air Force prisoners, are referred to the Group each year through prisoner screening boards at their home bases, or at the direction of courts-martial reviewing authorities at major air command or Headquarters USAF level. All of these airmen have requested to come to the Retraining Group. The great majority of Retrainees present a clinical picture of the character and behavior disorders of varying types and severity, with the immature and passive-aggressive personalities being most common.

All Retrainees assigned to Amarillo have been sentenced by court-martial to confinement. Their sentence may also include one or all of the following: withdrawal of rating, forfeiture of pay and allowances, and a punitive discharge. Approximately one-half of the Retrainees arrive with a Bad Conduct or Dishonorable Discharge in their sentence. The Group provides these Retrainees with an opportunity to prevent the stigma such a discharge would carry.

The major percentage of the offenses committed by the Retrainees continues to be those involving absence, dishonesty or fraud, and violence. These categories accounted for 78.3 percent of all Retrainees during calendar year 1964 (Table 2). Although airmen convicted of such serious crimes as narcotics usage, arson, rape, and murder are normally prohibited by regulation from coming to the Retraining Group, exceptions may and have been made.

2. Distribution of Retrainees by Major Offense Categories, 1964

Categories		Number	Percent
1. Absence		143	29.0
AWOL	142		
Desertion	1		
2. Dishonesty or Fraud		206	41.8
Forgery	7		
Larceny	164		
Postal Offenses	3		
Wrongful Appropriation	32		
3. Sex		15	3.0
4. Violence		37	7.5
Assault	21		
Aggravated Assault	2		
Unlawful Entry	12		
Manslaughter	1		
Robbery	1		
5. Against Authority and Breach of Discipline		42	8.5
Escape	3		
Insubordination	15		
Breaking Restriction	4		
Other	20		
6. Disorderly Conduct		31	6.3
Narcotics Violations	11		
Others	20		
7. Dereliction of Duty and Abuse of Authority		19	3.9
Total		493	100.0

Many people are surprised to learn that the Retrainees travel to Amarillo on commercial transportation and without escort. In many instances this travel involves thousands of miles and many days. Coming to the Retraining Group unescorted is, of course, a vital beginning to the program of rehabilitation. The fact that the annual rate of AWOL enroute to the Group averages only 1 percent attests to the motivation of the Retrainees.

Organization of the Retraining Group

The Retraining Group staff consists of 120 officers, airmen, and civilians, and includes a diversified background of skills and training. The organizational structure closely resembles a normal nontactical Air Force unit. There are four basic Divisions within the Group operating under the direction of the Commander:

1] The Chief of the Operations and Training Division also serves as the Deputy Commander. He is the central coordinator and administrator for the day-to-day operations of the Retraining Group. This includes both the programming for and the progress of individual Retrainees, as well as broader problems of the Group's operation. The Team Leaders, whose function we shall describe later, are assigned to this Division as is the Psychiatrist.

2] The Supervisory Division is responsible for the welfare, housing, custody, and discipline of the Retrainees. This Division is directed by an Air Police officer, and is composed predominantly of airmen and NCO's drawn from the Security and Law Enforcement career fields. The members of this Division have the most contact with and effect on the Retrainees after the normal duty hours.

3] The Educational Services Division is responsible for all Group training programs including academic training, vocational training, and attitude development and adjustment. This Division is composed of five civilian instructors who have experience teaching in correctional settings, plus military personnel drawn from the Educational and Training career fields.

4] The Analysis Division combines the research and clinical and counseling psychological services of the Retraining

Group. The three Branches of this Division are the Data Collection/Processing Branch, the Program Evaluation Branch, and the Psychological Services Branch.

Other Branches and functions are listed on the organizational chart, but these are self-explanatory and/or of secondary importance to the basic operating Divisions noted above.

The Treatment Teams

The Retraining Group launched a major innovation in program technique during the Fall of 1962. The basic change involved the elimination of Initial and Reclassification Boards and the establishment of Treatment Teams. A shorter period of confinement available for an increasing number of Retrainees was the precipitating factor behind the technique change. Air Force Regulation 125-2, published 1 March 1960, had lowered from ninety to the present sixty the minimum number of days remaining of a prisoner's confinement time upon entry into the Retraining Group.

The Retraining Group currently has three Treatment Teams, each of which is headed by a civilian Correctional Treatment Specialist. The Team Leaders have educational backgrounds in psychology and/or sociology. Other members of the Team include a representative from the Psychological Services Branch, a civilian instructor from the Educational Services Division, a military Vocational Training Specialist, and several Supervisory Division NCO Counselors.

Immediately upon arrival at the Group, the Retrainees are randomly assigned to a Team. The Team is in charge of the Retrainee throughout his stay in the Group. The Retrainees assigned to each Team are housed in separate barracks.

Within two weeks after his arrival, the Retrainee has his initial meeting with the full Team. The Team uses the information obtained from previous interviews with the Team Leader and other members of the Team, the results of psychological testing, and data from other sources to plan a tentative treatment program based on the Retrainee's particular needs. Since the Team meeting can be an extremely threatening experience for the Retrainee, every effort is made to provide a relaxed atmosphere.

The Retrainee is assigned primary and secondary counselors who will meet with him weekly, and who will carry the major counseling and therapy responsibility for guiding him through the program. In cases where denial of social reality or other forms of resistance are encountered, these counselors are able to confront the Retrainee with knowledge of his actual performance in specific situations.

Throughout the Retraining Group program there are frequent opportunities for interaction between the Retrainee and the Team members. The academic instructors have day-to-day contact with the Retrainee during the academic phase of the program. The Vocational Training Specialist may aid the Retrainee in working out adjustment problems in his career field or at his job outlet. The Supervisory NCO's offer day-to-day guidance in the barracks living areas. These NCO Counselors are particularly helpful in offering practical guidance about immediate problems and in aiding the Retrainee to adapt to the expectations of social reality.

Consultative and ancillary services are available to aid the Teams in planning a program of rehabilitation. The Clinical Psychologists may perform projective testing; the Retrainee may be referred to the Group's Psychiatrist for evaluation and/or therapy; advanced group therapy may be used; the Chaplains may provide counseling in the spiritual or moral areas; or the Base Staff Judge Advocate's Office may provide legal assistance. An active recreation program, under the direction of professional staff, is also available.

The Teams continue to meet with the Retrainee every two to four weeks, the frequency depending on the needs of the individual Retrainee. These meetings are used to coordinate all available information concerning the Retrainee, and to discuss any areas that the Retrainee or the Team feel require discussion.

The Treatment Teams are the heart of the Retraining Group's multidisciplinary approach to prisoner rehabilitation. Periodic evaluations have all concluded that, although several problems have existed in the day-to-day operation of the Team program, the Treatment Teams have clearly demonstrated their value as a therapeutic tool:

> Under the Team Treatment system, Retrainees meet the staff earlier, and interaction is more frequent and direct, of greater depth, and occurs over a longer period of time than was the case during the Board system. The effect of assigning a Retrainee to a Team from the moment of admission to completion of his program provides for a unified approach in programming and treatment . . . Team members can check the validity of their individual assessments of a particular case and gain the benefit of each other's observations of the Retrainee over a more continuous period of time than available to a single staff member (Hart, 1964).

The Retraining Group Program

The Retraining Group program begins with seven days of reception, orientation, and evaluation called Phase I. This consists of interviews with and lectures by various division and branch representatives, psychological testing, informal group discussions, and meetings with individual Team members.

The Retrainees then enter Phase II which lasts three weeks and is called Attitude Development and Adjustment. These three weeks consist primarily of classroom discussion groups on such topics as military conduct, citizenship, finances, personal hygiene, marriage and the family, legal affairs, and personality development. Group therapy sessions are also given considerable emphasis during this Phase.

All of the Retrainees who arrive at the Group during the same week progress together during Phases I and II. With Phase III, however, the Retrainees enter varied programs based on their individual abilities, skills, and needs.

Phase III consists of academic and/or vocational training. All Retrainees who have not graduated from high school, or who score lower than 10.5 on the California Achievement Test, are required to attend a four-week course of academic instruction conducted by the Educational Services Division. This course consists of the fundamentals of high school reading, writing, and arithmetic, and includes a speed-reading course employing tachistoscopic film-projection equipment.

Following the academic course, or if he does not attend academics, the Retrainee goes out onto the Base for vocational training. Many of the Retrainees were in a career field for which they were well-suited and to which regulations permit them to return. These Retrainees are placed in a job outlet in their career field on the Base and work at this job until they leave the Retraining Group. Most job outlets at Amarillo AFB are happy to accept Retrainees as they are characteristically quite good workers.

There are other Retrainees whose court-martial conviction prevents them from returning to their old career fields due to security regulations. Others were in career fields that the Retraining Group finds were not properly matched to their abilities. Such a Retrainee will enter an On-the-Job Training program in a new career field, or he will be entered as an overload student in one of the technical training courses offered at Amarillo AFB.

Following one month in Phase III, selected Retrainees are eligible to advance to Phase IV. Phase IV is an Honor Phase characterized by an increasing number of privileges and additional freedom of activities on the Base. The selection for advancement to Phase IV is made by a Board of Supervisory NCO's, and is based upon such factors as military bearing, discipline, attitude, progress in training, and performance in the Group area.

As the Retrainee moves toward completion of his program, the Team prepares a recommendation for discharge or restoration which will be considered by a Classification Board composed of military officers. This Board reviews the Retrainee's progress in the Group, hears a brief summary from the Team Leader, and then interviews the Retrainee. Although the Board typically agrees with the recommendation of the Team, the Board does have the authority to challenge or even reverse the Team's recommendation. The decision of the Classification Board is then reviewed by the Group Commander and approved by higher authorities as may be required.

The Retrainees move to Phase V when they have completed the confinement portion of their sentences. Phase V Retrainees thus have the same privileges as full-duty airmen, including complete freedom of the Base and the surrounding communities. Most of the Retrainees in Phase V have already met the Classification Board and are awaiting reassignment to another Base or separation from the Air Force. In calendar year 1964 the Retrainees spent an average of 100.2 days in the Retraining Group program, with the range being 30–290 days.

Results

The Analysis Division of the Retraining Group conducts continuing follow-up studies of all Retrainees restored to duty. Questionnaires are sent to the Squadron Commander of each restoree six months after he leaves the Retraining Group. These questionnaires provide quantitative and qualitative information concerning the airman's progress. Other data is obtained later to determine in what manner the restorees complete their military commitment.

The Retraining Group is quite proud of the results. During fiscal year 1964 the Retraining Group restored to duty 312 (66.1 percent) of the 472 Retrainees who completed the program. The six-month follow-up of these restorees showed that 85.5 percent had served in an acceptable manner during that period of time and could be considered "Short-Term Successes." *

During calendar year 1963† 318 Retrainees were restored to duty. Follow-up studies show that 263 (82.7 percent) were "Long-Term Successes" in that they performed satisfactorily in the Air Force, and were discharged Honorably or Under Honorable Conditions during or at the completion of their remaining military commitment.

Equally as important as the quantitative results of the

---

* "Failures" include those who committed a serious offense during this period and were discharged from the Air Force under conditions other than Honorable and/or those being considered for discharge.

† Since the average length of time remaining on a Retrainee's current enlistment at the time he leaves the Retraining Group is thirty months, these are the latest statistics available on "Long-Term Success."

program is the quality of service the restorees perform for the
Air Force. The Squadron Commanders' six-month ratings of
Retrainees restored to duty during fiscal year 1964 indicate that
87.8 percent were considered to have performed "Average"
(36.6 percent) and "Above Average" (51.2 percent), while only
12.2 percent were rated "Below Average."

Conclusions

The relatively high degree of success of the 3320th Retraining Group has attracted the interest of both military and
civilian correctional personnel. This success appears to be based
on the multidisciplinary Therapeutic Community approach
utilizing Treatment Teams. These Teams provide, within the
limits of the resources of the Group, a maximum opportunity
for each Retrainee to shed his unhealthy patterns of social behavior and to begin functioning in a manner more acceptable
to the setting to which he will return.

Numerous recent reports in the literature indicate that
individuals who live in a meaningful and therapeutic relationship, even for a relatively limited period of time, show profound
and significant changes in personality, attitudes, and behavior.
The Retraining Group is a Therapeutic Community in this
sense. It is a healthy and realistic community wherein the Retrainee can relearn his self-image, and develop new communication and role-playing skills which will allow more adequate
growth and permit the maximum realization of individual
potential.

The present framework of policies and procedures used
in the Retraining Group are not, however, accepted in any final
sense. They are constantly being reviewed, challenged, evaluated, and altered. Supporting this attitude of change is a continuing research effort by the entire staff. Experimentation and
validation of new approaches and techniques is a continuing
challenge of the Retraining Group.

Although the Retraining Group operates in the limited
sphere of the *military* offender, such an approach to the reha-

bilitation of the maladaptive individuals in our society can probably be effectively adopted by other military and civilian organizations having similar missions.

II

RESTORATION TO DUTY

7

Selection for Restoration, Clemency, and Parole: An Examination of the Decision-Making Process

STANLEY L. BRODSKY

Who is the military restoree? From the tens of thousands of individuals sentenced to military confinement yearly, how are decisions made to select for this alternative of rejoining the military services? In the first chapter the events and choice points leading up to confinement, the screening procedures, and the nature of military justice were considered. In the chapters by Broder, Gray, and Mooney, the retraining procedures, success rates and characteristics of restored servicemen were reported. The present chapter seeks to fill the gap between the confinement decision and the actual restoration-to-duty action and its aftermath. In addition criteria related to the other two early release possibilities of the military prisoner—clemency and parole—are discussed.

A key theoretical factor in restoration, clemency, and parole decision-making is the psychological appropriateness of return to duty or early release. Clinical evaluations by social workers, clinical psychologists, and psychiatrists are administered to military prisoners routinely and yes-no recommendations are submitted as part of the outcome of the evaluation. The present goals are to focus on the psychiatric evaluations with respect to two other key components in decision-making, classification board recommendations, and prisoner status as discharged or not-discharged, and to study how they related to the criterion of final Department of Army action in Washington. This was intended primarily to provide baseline information on the interaction between psychiatric status of the prisoner and prisoner disposition. Most military psychiatrists are transitory and typically not part of the military command or power structure. Thus the study yielded data about the discrepancy between perceptions of these transient officers and Army actions. The information examined is derived primarily from Army facilities; however the data seem to be representative of military-wide events and results.

OTHER STUDIES

In a study of 920 U.S. Disciplinary Barracks (USDB) punitively-discharged prisoners, Cook (1960) tabulated psychiatric recommendations for return to duty and Washington action on restoration to duty during the period 1957–59. About 15 percent of the total subjects were restored and considerably fewer recommended. Sixty-one percent of those recommended for restoration were restored, while 91 percent of those not recommended for restoration were not restored. These data are shown in Table 3.

3. Psychiatric Recommendations and Return to Duty by Washington Action

	Cook (1960)			Mooney (1964)		
Recommendations	Yes	No	Subtotal	Yes	No	Subtotal
Yes	46	30	76	10	0	10
No	73	771	844	5	25	30
Total	119	801	920	15	25	40

Mooney (1964) studied psychiatric recommendations and Washington action in 107 punitively-discharged USDB prisoners. He eliminated forty-four of these subjects from his investigation because they did not desire restoration, and twenty-three more were omitted because of the presence of some of the following "stop" items (a variable associated *only* with non-restored subjects) in their records: less than seven months military service, military grade below E-2, less than nineteen years old, a sentence over twenty-four months, or a homosexual offense or sexual offense involving minors. For the forty remaining cases, the results are presented in Table 3. All ten of the subjects who had been recommended were restored and twenty-five of the thirty with negative recommendations were not restored.

The difference between the Cook and Mooney studies are exaggerated as a result of the elimination by Mooney of many subjects that were not restored who would have been included in the Cook study. Similarities are present in the relatively high incidences of negative psychiatric recommendations and negative restoration actions.

The Present Study

The purpose was to explore the relationship of psychiatric and other recommendations at the USDB to final decisions about restoration, clemency, and parole. The data were extracted from 273 Army prisoner records completed in spring, 1966. The recommendations and actions referred only to the latest consideration and remissions of forfeitures of pay were not included as clemency actions. When the institutional board votes were not unanimous, the majority decisions were counted. The time sequence of occurrence of the recommendations and actions was as follows: Psychiatrist, Restoration Officer, Institutional Board, and Washington action. The psychiatric recommendation was based on cumulative information based on social histories, psychological testing, and mental status examination.

The number of subjects falling in each category—restoration, clemency, and parole—was variable since all prisoners were considered for clemency, while some never became eligible for parole due to short sentences, and others were not considered for restoration.

Results

RESTORATION

The results were tabulated separately for punitively-discharged and no-discharge prisoners. Relatively few of the subjects were psychiatrically recommended for restoration: 29 of 147 in the discharged group were recommended and 7 of 47 in the no-discharge group. Approximately the same proportion of discharged prisoners were recommended by the institutional board and a higher proportion—12 of 47—of the no-discharge prisoners.

Favorable actions were taken on restoration for 6 of 147 of discharged prisoners, but all six cases were associated with *yes* recommendations by both the psychiatrist and the board. Fifteen other instances of psychiatrist and board *yes* agreement coincided with negative restoration action. Factors related to return to duty of no-discharge prisoners appeared to be quite different. Twenty-five subjects were separated from the service and all received a board and a psychiatric *no*. Such an agreement did not necessarily mean separation, however, for ten individuals who fell in this category were indeed returned to duty. All of the remaining twelve prisoners who had received psychiatric and/or board *yes* were returned to duty.

A comparative listing of psychiatric recommendations and restoration actions is presented in Table 4. In addition to the studies already noted, a report from the Ft. Knox stockade of no-discharge prisoners is included (Blackman, Speshock, and Boyd, 1963). A consistently low rate of positive psychiatric recommendation for restoration was present, ranging from 8 percent in the Cook study to 38 percent in the Blackman study. The amount of agreement of action with recommendations was generally high. The two exceptions both reflected general policy decisions.

In the study of the restoration data, one further variable was considered. The restoration officer, a civilian also involved in classification decisions, made a *yes* or *no* recommendation on return to duty. Substantial agreement was present between restoration officer recommendations and those of the psychiatrist and the board. Only those punitively-discharged prisoners who were favorably recommended by everyone were returned and only those no-discharge prisoners negatively recommended by everyone were not returned.

4. Restoration Recommendations and Actions by Special Studies

Authors	Population	Number		Percent		
				Yes Psychiatric Recommendation	Agreement of Action with Yes Recommendation	Agreement of Action with No Recommendation
Cook (1960)	USDB Prisoners	920	Punitive Discharge	8	61	91
Mooney (1964)	USDB Prisoners	40	Punitive Discharge	25	100	83
Present Study[1] (1966)	USDB Prisoners	47	No Discharge	15	100	63
Present Study (1966)	USDB Prisoners	147	Punitive Discharge	20	21	100
Blackman, S., Speshock, M. J., and Boyd, R. C. (1963)	Stockade Prisoners	47[2]	No Discharge	38	72	41

[1] Present studies were made by Stanley L. Brodsky.
[2] Includes 12 subjects with "Doubtful" recommendations.

CLEMENCY AND PAROLE

Considerably different results emerged when the same procedures of comparing recommendations and actions were performed for clemency and parole. A reduction of sentence was granted in 41 of the 92 times recommended by a psychiatrist and in 37 of the 80 times recommended by the board. In the 178 negative actions 127 had been recommended by a psychiatrist and 135 by the institutional board.

The parole findings represent the greatest agreement between recommendations and action. Agreement with positive recommendations occurred in 44 of 78 psychiatric recommendations and 45 of 62 board recommendations. Only three individuals with negative psychiatric recommendations were given parole and only two with negative board recommendations. Parole was granted a total of 47 times in the 162 cases considered.

Discussion

The purpose of this study was to examine the patterns of actions and recommendations on restoration, clemency, and parole. It was found that a paradoxical pattern appeared in restoration recommendations for the discharge and no-discharge prisoners. Whereas for punitively-discharged prisoners any *no* recommendation from any source seemed to preclude restoration, for no-discharge prisoners any *yes* recommendation seemed to insure return to duty. A very low number of punitively-discharged prisoners were restored, while almost half of the no-discharge prisoners were returned to duty. Overall it was found that approximately one-sixth of the prisoners were restored to military duty and that clemency and parole actions were approved in one-third of the cases.

Clemency recommendations were found to be minimally associated with final actions while parole recommendations were strongly associated with parole being granted. In the three categories considered, the differences between recommending sources was slight compared to the overall differences between recommendations and actions. The board, psychiatrist, restoration officer, and other local personnel seemed to be more in agreement with each other than with Washington actions. Thus the issue is somewhat revolved of the consonance of the psychiatrist, who is only transient with the military, with the military structure. The "fit" was good in the prison itself and fair with the central military decision-making organization.

A brief observation needs to be added about the bases for psychiatric and institutional recommendations. These are founded primarily on clinical and discursive information. The decision for clemency is sometimes recommended, for example, because a prisoner is too psychologically ill to benefit from further incarceration or because he is psychologically healthy and does not need incarceration. A prisoner may not be recommended for restoration because he states he does not wish to return, or in the case of non-discharged prisoners, may be restored for the very same reason. The local consensus is a result in part of accessibility to identical data by the varying parties and of sequential decisions, and not indicative of predictive, empirical information. There is a need to undertake predictive validity studies so that such military correctional decision-making may be objectively and quantitatively based.

8

Characteristics of Restorees

BERNARD L. MOONEY

One of the primary functions of the United States Disciplinary Barracks (USDB) is the rehabilitation of its inmates in preparing them for possible return to active military duty. On a simple intuitive basis, it has been felt that inmates actually approved for return to duty are a homogeneous group distinct from inmates not approved for restoration. No clear-cut evidence exists to indicate the characteristics which distinguish restorees nor, for that matter, that restorees actually are a distinct group.

A study completed by the USDB Council for Research and Evaluation (Grabein, Tapogna, and Mooney, 1964) indicated that potential restorees could be distinguished from potential non-restorees on the basis of several quantifiable life-history variables including: tested level of education, highest military grade held, and total length of military service. Potential restorees were shown to possess higher levels of these several variables in contrast with non-restorees. However, these potential restorees were inmates selected for inclusion in a Special Training Program as preparation for return to duty either because they had received no punitive discharge or because, in the opinion of the Special Training Program staff, they were good candidates for eventual return to duty. This group of potential restorees did not represent all inmates selected for return to duty nor were all these potential restorees eventually restored to duty.

Within the 3320th Retraining Group, Amarillo Air Force Base, Texas (Hippchen and O'Donnell, 1962) indications were found that life-history variables clearly distinguished between group of restored and non-restored Air Force prisoners. Amarillo's results are highly similar to those obtained with USDB potential restorees and non-restorees. Within the Amarillo Retraining Group, restorees were older and exhibited higher levels of education, greater length of total service, and higher military rank.

Life-history variables of the type thus far cited have frequently been referred to as static. In other words, these variables either refer to facts or events established prior to confinement or refer to qualities of the inmate which are fixed and not amenable to alteration through an institutional program, e.g., an inmate's marital status, age, or his level of intelligence. It has been argued that such variables cannot reflect the alterations and changes which occur during an inmate's progress through the confinement situation. This argument insists that more individualized and more dynamic measures of change are imperative in assessing the eventual outcome of confinement. However, facts drawn from the life history of the individual may be considered as representing the end product of interaction among many dynamic factors constituting stable, component parts of the personality. In this sense, it has been argued that the predictive power of such life-history variables is probably superior to that of the supposedly more dynamic variables derived from sources such as psychological testing.

The purpose of the present study is to investigate possible differences between groups of actually restored prisoners and non-restored prisoners from the USDB on the basis of the types of life-history variables thus far described. Beyond the consideration of the life-history or static variables previously employed in research of this type, the present study proposes to consider a dynamic variable which will include an evaluation of the inmate's current overall adjustment. It represents a synthesis of a thoroughgoing psychiatric interview with the inmate and involves a summation of the inmate's total liabilities and assets from a psychiatric standpoint.

The research hypotheses to be tested in the present study are twofold. Based on previous findings, the first hypothesis is directional in nature and stated empirically is: Restored prisoners will exhibit higher levels of the variables pertaining to age, length of service, and military grade in contrast with non-restored prisoners. The second hypothesis is non-directional in nature and includes those variables for which no consistent replicated findings are available in this area. The second hypothesis is stated empirically as: Significant differences will exist between restored and non-restored prisoners in the variables of type of offense, branch of service, number of prior civilian and military offenses, length of sentence to confinement and psychiatric recommendation.

Methods and Materials

SUBJECTS

A random sample of 123 cases were collected. It was composed of inmates received into the USDB between October and December 1962. Data on nine life-history or static variables as well as the one dynamic variable were extracted from the records for each inmate. Five cases were dropped for lack of sufficient data.

MATERIALS

The nine static variables selected for consideration were: *1]* age upon arrival at the USDB; *2]* length of creditable military service prior to confinement; *3]* highest military grade held; *4]* type of offense, i.e., strictly military offenses, offenses against property or offenses against a person of either an assaultive or sexual nature; *5]* branch of military service, i.e., Army or Air Force; *6]* number of prior civilian offenses described as felonies; *7]* number of prior military courts-martial; *8]* length of sentence of confinement; *9]* General Technical Aptitude Area score from the Army Classification Battery. The tenth variable was the psychiatric recommendation relative to restoration.

PROCEDURES

After a period of approximately nine months, data regarding Washington decisions on Classification Board recommendations regarding restoration were obtained for each case. In several cases, multiple considerations for restoration had been
given. In these instances, the most recent Washington decisions
were considered as the definition of restored versus non-restored.

It was evident that two administratively distinct types of
cases were represented among those eventually restored to duty
from the USDB. The first type was those inmates whose sentence
by the military court-martial included a punitive discharge. The
second type was those inmates whose sentence either did not
include a punitive discharge or who received a suspended punitive discharge. Of a total of eleven such cases, two were denied
restoration and recommended for administrative separation
from the service. Further investigation of the records revealed
that in the latter cases, the two inmates had indicated they had
no desire to return to duty. Since, in cases of no discharge or
suspended punitive discharges, restoration to duty depends little
on evaluation of the inmate and represents more an automatic
administrative procedure, it was decided to exclude these cases
from consideration.

Of the 107 cases that remained, 44 inmates (41%) indicated
a desire not to return to duty and none of these were restored to
duty. Consequently, these cases were dropped, leaving a total
of 63 cases with punitive discharges indicating a desire to return
to duty. Of this number, 15 were approved for return to duty
by Washington and 48 were disapproved.

RESULTS

Following initial tabulation of the several variables for
each case, it was readily apparent that "stop" items or empty
cells existed among the data, i.e., the presence or absence of a
given variable or of a clearly defined level of a variable was

associated only with the non-restored group and never occurred in any of the cases restored to duty. The "stop" items are the following: *1*] less than seven months creditable military service prior to confinement; *2*] military grade below Private, E-2; *3*] less than nineteen years of age at time of confinement; *4*] a sentence to confinement in excess of twenty-four months; *5*] a homosexual offense or a sexual offense involving minors. Since the presence of one or more of these "stop" items in an inmate's record was consistently associated with non-restoration, the twenty-three cases exhibiting these "stop" items were excluded from the statistical analyses which follow.

As a group the restored prisoners were significantly older and had rendered significantly longer creditable military service than the non-restored group. The mean age of the restored group was 26.7 years and that of the non-restored group was 21.5 years. The restored subjects served a mean of 75.7 months of honorable military duty and the non-restored subjects, 30.2 months. Because of the markedly unequal variances in the two groups, the Mann-Whitney U test was employed to test the significance of the mean differences.

The mean scores on a measure of general mental ability, the General Technical Aptitude Area of the Army Classification Battery, were 108.5 for the restored group and 96.9 for the non-restored group. The mean of the restored group was significantly higher. Approximately 93 percent of the restored group had scores of 90 or higher; in the non-restored group 36 percent achieved scores below 90, evidencing below average general mental ability.

The distributions were tabulated in the restored and non-restored groups for the variables of military branch and grade, offense type, and prior civilian and military offenses. Chi square values were calculated and none of these five variables was distributed differently between the two groups at the .05 level of significance.

When the same procedure was followed for the variable of psychiatric recommendations, ten positive and five negative recommendations were found in the restored group. No positive recommendations and twenty-five negative ones were found in the non-restored group.

Application of the Chi Square test to the psychiatric recommendations data yielded a value for chi square of 18.81 (p < .001). These findings indicate a highly significant difference in final disposition of cases between those cases receiving positive psychiatric recommendations and those receiving negative recommendations. It should be pointed out here that undoubtedly the psychiatric recommendations are not and cannot be considered as formed entirely apart from life-history information of the type treated thus far in the present study. For example, positive psychiatric recommendations are infrequently given in cases where evidence of limited mental abilities is found. From the psychiatric standpoint, such individuals often do not possess the necessary resources to enable them to respond adequately to the demands of active military service. Thus, the significance of psychiatric recommendations in regard to final disposition of cases is based in part on the fact that the psychiatric recommendation represents a summation of the individual's assets and liabilities for further active duty.

Discussion of Results

The first hypothesis of the study was supported by the findings regarding only the age and length of service variables. These findings, that the restored group was significantly older than the non-restored Group, and has significantly longer periods of prior military service, are largely compatible. One would expect that individuals having longer periods of service are also chronologically older. However, the finding of no significant superiority of the restored over the non-restored Group in military rank is somewhat surprising, especially in view of the earlier findings within the USDB (Grabein, Tapogna, and Mooney, 1964) and Amarillo (Hippchen & O'Donnell, 1962). Consideration was given to the possibility that exclusion of individuals in grade E-1 (Recruit) may have unduly influenced results. However, of twelve such individuals, ten expressed a desire not to return to duty, thus eliminating them from consideration. Inclusion of the remaining two in the computations for the Chi Square Test did not alter the results.

In regard to the several "stop" items, it is interesting to

note that the Amarillo findings, though not structured in the same fashion, do parallel the present results. It was determined that being seventeen to eighteen years of age, having less than twelve months total military service, and holding the rank of Airman Basic (equivalent to Army grade E-1 Recruit) was associated with a significantly below average probability of being restored to active duty (Hippchen & O'Donnell, 1962). The marked similarity between their latter findings and "stop" items, numbers *1*, *2*, and *3*, of the present study as well as the consistency of the findings regarding age and length of service have important implications for those in the field of military corrections. The results point up the unacceptability for further active duty of the young, relatively inexperienced serviceman who has been convicted of violations of military law.

There is no clear evidence from the present study that the factors of youth and limited military experience are associated with other factors which, per se, are impediments to further military duty as for example, moral turpitude, when defined as number of prior civilian or military convictions. It is possible that the principle: "The past is the best predictor of the future" is operational in this matter, i.e., the older, experienced serviceman has his prior military record to support him whereas the younger man has a very limited military record to point up his capacity to respond adequately to the demands inherent in military service. On the other hand, it may be valid to assume that the individual who violates the military legal code early in his military career has thereby demonstrated an essential resistance to the regimen of military service. Both interpretations appear assumptions warranting further exploration.

Apart from "stop" item number five, regarding homosexual offenses or sex offenses with minors, there were no significant differences between the groups regarding type of confining offenses. These findings are not in agreement with those obtained in the Amarillo project (Hippchen & O'Donnell, 1962). However, the USDB, unlike Amarillo, is a confinement facility. Actual military retraining involves only those approved for return to duty by Washington. Retraining is handled outside the confines of the USDB. It is quite possible that the individuals convicted of assaultive and sexual offenses and sent to

Amarillo specifically for military retraining, differ in important respects from those convicted of the same offense and sent to the USDB primarily for confinement.

The results of the analyses performed regarding branch of service, and number of prior civilian and military offenses revealed no significant differences between groups. In regard to prior civilian offenses, there is close screening which occurs prior to induction or enlistment into the armed forces so that generally individuals with a large number of civilian offenses on record would not be accepted by the military. Prior military offenses were defined as number of military courts-martial received prior to the court-martial which remanded the individual to the USDB. However, in many cases, individuals had received several courts-martial with suspended sentences (e.g., for repeated AWOLs) which were vacated and included in the sentence given by the court-martial remanding the person to the USDB. For the present study, such cases were categorized as having had no prior courts-martial. It can only be conjectured whether straightforward tabulation of number of discrete appearances before a military court-martial, regardless of sentencing, would yield results different from those obtained.

A finding, unexpected on the basis of earlier results, was that of a significant superiority of the restored over the nonrestored group on the General Technical Aptitude Area score of the Army Classification Battery. Nevertheless, these results are in keeping with trends in research findings regarding the relationship between GTAA score and military effectiveness. A study of the score distributions suggests that the obtained differences were less the result of selecting only those with unusually high scores but more the result of excluding those with below average scores.

Finally, a most striking difference was observed between the restored and non-restored groups in regard to the psychiatric recommendations for restoration. Out of the ten individuals given positive recommendations, 100 percent were returned to duty. Of the thirty individuals who received negative recommendations, only 17 percent were eventually returned to duty. No other single factor in the study produced as efficient discrimination between groups.

9

Evaluation of the Army's Restoration Program

JOHN MORRIS GRAY

The policy of the Department of the Army is to promote the rehabilitation of prisoners with two possible ends in view; namely, the restoration to duty of those qualified so that they may earn honorable discharges, and the preparation of those not restored for return to civil life. The Provost Marshal General, under the general staff supervision of the Deputy Chief of Staff for Personnel, has Army staff responsibility for the Army Correction Program, to include restoration, clemency, and parole for military prisoners.

A committee appointed by Secretary of the Army Brucker to study and report on the effectiveness of the Uniform Code of Military Justice and its bearing on good order and discipline within the Army, reaffirmed in its 1960 report the principles which are common to the administration of military justice and the treatment of offenders throughout the Army. These are:

> The entire system of sentences under the Uniform Code of Military Justice is an open-end system. There is opportunity, generally regardless of the length of the sentence, for an individual to demonstrate his worthiness for restoration to honorable service. It is a prime concern of the Army that each offender be encouraged to make use of this opportunity.

A significant finding of the committee was "The Army has a superior system for screening, rehabilitating, and restoring prisoners in confinement." It is noteworthy that there have been no substantial changes in procedures, or in the system for restoration of prisoners to duty since the publication of this committee report (The Powell Report) in January, 1960. Equally noteworthy is the fact that there has been no recent attempt to evaluate the adjustment to the Army of prisoners restored to an honorable duty status. It is to this end that this study is directed.

The methodology of this study utilized both the survey and analytical research methods. A list of prisoners restored to duty by Department of the Army action from January 1958 through June 1964 was compiled in the Office of The Provost Marshal General. Information as to the type of offense committed, where it occurred, and the approximate date of the offense was obtained from the Office of the Judge Advocate General. The Office of the Adjutant General supplied pertinent information from the personnel records of the restored prisoners. A survey was conducted by the use of a mail questionnaire to the current unit commanders of the restored prisoners. The time of the mail survey included the period of 15 July 1964 to 15 December 1964.

Introduction

"It is the policy of the Department of Defense that discipline be administered on a corrective rather than a punitive basis, and that military places of confinement be administered on a uniform basis" (Department of Defense Instruction, Number 1325.4, 1955). With this general policy statement the Department of Defense sets the standard for today's modern military correctional system. The directive establishing this standard goes into considerable detail as to the provisions to be made for the rehabilitation of military prisoners and includes a specific requirement that measures be provided to prepare for successful return to duty those prisoners whose sentences do not include punitive discharges and those with sentences including punitive discharges who are considered potentially restorable. Prisoners of potential value to the military service, who have been sentenced to punitive discharges and whose return to duty will not adversely affect the esprit and good name of the service, should be restored upon completion of any restoration training provided. Each service is enjoined to provide restoration training for its own personnel with a course of instruction based on the military training program of that service. Programs are to include rehabilitative instruction, intensive military training, and opportunities to prove their fitness to return to honorable duty. The following general criteria are established by the Department of Defense to be used as a guide for selecting prisoners for participation in restoration programs:

1] A sincere desire for restoration and demonstrated motivation for military service.

2] Mental and physical fitness for military service.

3] An absence of criminal and antisocial characteristics.

4] An absence of any factors which in the event of restoration, would adversely affect the esprit and good name of the service.

5] In the absence of exceptional circumstances, conviction of a major offense generally recognized as a felony in the civil courts should ordinarily preclude selection for restoration training. "Exceptional circumstances" should include such factors as youth, a comparatively low degree of turpitude or wrongful intent in the commission of the offense, a substantially clear civil and military record with a reputation of honesty and good behavior prior to the commission of the current offense and demonstrated or potential ability to perform military duties in a creditable manner.

Army regulations prescribed the policy and procedures for the restoration of military prisoners sentenced to confinement and discharge (AR 600-332). These regulations are in complete accord with the Department of Defense policy as stated above and are readily available to Army personnel with a need to know; therefore, specific provisions will not be cited here. Since the basic purpose of this study is to evaluate the effectiveness of the Army's restoration program, perhaps a brief look into achievements in the past might lend depth to the overall evaluation.

Background Information*

The United States Army has long performed the dual role of jailer and rehabilitation agent for people sentenced by courts-martial to terms of confinement. In times of peace, the Army prisoner population has occasionally dwindled to hundreds. In time of war, the Army has operated a correctional and confinement system larger than the Federal Prison System. In January, 1940, there were only 759 punitive discharge prisoners in the Army confinement facilities. This population reached a peak of almost 35,000 (34,766) in October 1945, and it decreased to 8,940 by December 1948.

The offenses committed by these punitive-discharge prisoners ranged from the purely military offenses to the most heinous felonies, which are severely punished under all enlightened systems of law, both civil and military. Offenders ranged from youths, not yet recovered from their first homesickness, to hardened criminals. There were officers, recruits, and

* The statistics pertaining to military prisoners included herein cover many different matters, involve large numbers of persons over a twenty-four-year period, and were obtained from many sources. Consequently, there are some discrepancies; however the statistical data presented is substantially correct. The primary sources of statistics are the following documents; unless otherwise credited, statistics were given to me from one of these sources:

a] *The Army Correctional System*, Office of the Adjutant General, Department of the Army, Washington, D.C., 2 January 1952.

b] *Monthly Statistical Reports*, Office of the Adjutant General, Correction Branch, Washington, D.C., April 1944 through June 1951.

c] *Semi-Annual Statistical Reports*, Office of the Adjutant General, Correction Branch, Department of the Army, Washington, D.C., January 1954 through December 1963.

d] *Semi-Annual Statistical Summaries*, Office of the Provost Marshal General, Department of the Army, Washington, D.C., January 1954 through July 1964.

e] Historical Monograph of the Correction Division, Adjutant General's Office: *A Report of the Army's Program for Military Prisoners in the Continental United States*. Volume I, November 1940 to August 1945; Volume II, September 1945 to December 1945.

f] *History of Department of the Army Activities Related to Korean Conflict*, Office of the Provost Marshal General, Department of the Army, Washington, D.C., 25 January 1950–8 September 1951.

g] *Activities of Office of the Provost Marshal General*, Department of the Army, Washington, D.C., 9 September 1951–31 December 1952.

h] *Summaries of Major Events and Problems* (RCS CSHIS-6), Office of the Provost Marshal General, Department of the Army, Washington, D.C., January 30–June 1953, and fiscal year reports thereafter, through fiscal year 1962.

combat-tested "noncoms"; there were the brilliant and the mentally dull; shirkers and workers; heroes and cowards. But they all possessed one thing in common: they had been convicted of serious violations of the criminal laws governing the armed forces of the United States.

The Army was charged with the mission of administering these prisoners, and it did so through the Army Correctional System, and its several types of confinement facilities. One facet of this mission was to see that the adjudged punishments, as reduced by clemency, parole, or restoration, were served. A second, and the one with which we are primarily concerned here, was to restore to honorable status in the Army all prisoners, regardless of their place of confinement, who gave evidence of their fitness for further service. Finally, with respect to those prisoners not considered suitable for restoration, the Army strove to provide a program of training which would contribute to their community adjustment and make them better citizens upon their return to civilian society.

The foundation of the present-day Army confinement and correctional program was laid with the passage of the Act of March 4, 1915, which provided that the United States Military Prison should thereafter be known as the United States Disciplinary Barracks, and that the government and control of that institution, its branches, and all offenders sent there should be vested in the Adjutant General, under the direction of the Secretary of War. The Act also provided authority for the granting of clemency and restoration. In 1947, the Secretary of the Army was substituted for the Secretary of War, and in 1950, the Act was amended to permit the Secretary to designate the branch, office, or officers of the Army who would govern this system. This function was performed by the Adjutant General of the Army from 1915, until August, 1954, when it was transferred to the Provost Marshal General.

The United States Disciplinary Barracks has long been the principle continuing military institution for the confinement of Army punitive-discharge prisoners, but in times of national emergency, the Army has also established procedures for rehabilitating and restoring punitive-discharge prisoners to duty. Many prisoners convicted of civilian type felonies and serious military offenses are transferred to Federal penal institutions. Punitive-discharge prisoners sentenced to short terms of confinement (normally six months or less) are confined in local stockades.

Restoration to duty and sentence reduction actions in cases of punitive-discharge prisoners in stockades are taken by the general courts-martial convening authorities who are vested with local command supervision over the stockades. Clemency, parole, and restoration actions in the cases of punitive-discharge prisoners confined in the U.S. Disciplinary Barracks and Federal institutions are centralized in Headquarters, Department of the Army. Although the Army Correctional System is administered for all prisoners, most of this study is devoted to restoration aspects of the program as it has affected punitive-discharge prisoners confined in places other than stockades. It spans a period of over twenty-four years and two major military conflicts in which this country has been embroiled.

WORLD WAR II AND THE POST-WAR DEMOBILIZATION PERIOD, 1940–50

Prior to World War II the Army had a single disciplinary barracks—The United States Disciplinary Barracks at Fort Leavenworth, Kansas. Between 1940 and 1950, fifteen branch disciplinary barracks were in operation at one time or another to accommodate the increased numbers of punitive-discharge prisoners. Additionally, in December 1942, rehabilitation centers were established in the nine service commands in the United States, and they operated until 1946, when the rapidly declining prisoner population rendered their continuance unnecessary.

Manpower was our most precious resource during the war years, and every possible effort was expended to rehabilitate the maximum number of general prisoners. The efficacy of the Army clemency, restoration, and rehabilitation programs is evident from the disposition of punitive-discharge prisoners at Army installations in the United States and overseas, and at Federal penal institutions from 1940, when the Army was mobilized, through December 1946:

Admissions:

Commitments, excluding transfers	84,245

Releases:

Restored to duty	42,373
Dishonorable Discharge	22,542
Honorable or Blue Discharge	792
Parole	1,793
Died	135
Other releases and separations	836
In confinement 31 December 1946	*15,774*

With the gradual scaling down of the Army's strength, the requirements for restoration to duty became increasingly stringent after June 1946, and there was a drastic decrease in both numbers and percentages of restorations to duty. Another reason for this decrease was the fact that practically all restorable men had been processed for restoration by that time.

The Army's wartime and postwar restoration program was a tremendous achievement from the administrative and training standpoint. However, it was most significant because of its underlying philosophy. It is notable that the number of men restored to duty was about the strength of three full infantry divisions. Even more notable is the fact that more than 42,000 men who had been sentenced to confinement, many for long terms, were not only released from confinement, but they were also given the chance to save themselves from the stigma and lifelong handicap of a dishonorable discharge.

This accomplishment is all the more significant in view of the fact that civil prisoners sentenced to penal and correctional institutions can never completely clear themselves of the stigma of conviction and imprisonment, even in those comparatively few cases where a full pardon is granted. The Army gave 50 percent of its World War II prisoners with punitive discharges a chance to return to honorable duty and thus virtually wipe out their convictions. While complete statistics are not available on what happened to these men after they were restored, it is known that 80 percent were rendering satisfactory service six months after restoration (MacCormick, 1947).

EFFECTS OF THE KOREAN HOSTILITIES, JUNE 1950–JUNE 1956

Much of the present Army Correctional System was in operation when the Korean conflict started in 1950, and "Korea" put it to a first severe test. In June 1950, the total active Army strength was down to 593,000 and there were 6,269 punitive-discharge prisoners in confinement as follows:

Disciplinary Barracks	2,985
Penitentiaries and other Federal Inst.	2,183
Stockades	651
Overseas	450
Total	*6,269*

Punitive-discharge confinements from 1 July 1950 through 30 June 1956, roughly covering the Korean mobilization and subsequent strength reduction, totaled approximately 43,000, of which about 31,700 were confined in disciplinary barracks. The movement of population in and out of disciplinary barracks for this six-year period (1 July 1950–30 June 1956) was as follows (to nearest 100):

Gains:		
Confined, 1 July 1950	2,600	
New confinements, 1 July 50—30 June 56	31,700	
Total Gains:		*34,300*
Restored to duty	1,800	
Paroled	5,800	
Expiration of sentence	18,000	
Transferred to Federal Inst.	3,000	
Escaped	100	
Transferred to retraining facilities	500	
Transferred to Navy Retraining Command	100	
Other releases	600	
Total Releases:		*29,900*
Confined, 30 June 56		*4,400*

The great majority of punitive-discharge prisoners not confined in disciplinary barracks or Federal institutions were confined in local stockades where clemency was exercised by the local general court-martial convening authority. This clemency included reduction or remission of confinement and forfeitures and, in many cases, restoration to duty. Nearly three thousand punitive-discharge prisoners in stockades were restored to duty from July 1950 through June 1956.

RECENT TRENDS:
Fiscal Years 1956–59

The bulk of the increased punitive-discharge prisoner population generated by the Korean conflict had been restored or released by June 1956. Although the more serious offenders from that period would continue in confinement for some time to come, the Army Correctional System was essentially on a peacetime basis. The Army strength was down to 1,026,000 on June 30th, 1956, and there were 6,442 punitive-discharge prisoners in confinement, a drop of more than fifteen hundred in one year.

A phenomenal reduction in the Disciplinary Barracks punitive-discharge population, 85 percent since the post-Korean peak in 1955, has resulted in the closing of four of the five disciplinary barracks. The disciplinary barracks at Fort Leavenworth, Kansas, with less than one thousand Army prisoners, is the only one now in operation. Only part of this reduction is due to a drop in Army strength. One major cause has been the emphasis on screening prisoners at *the stockade level* to weed out misfits and, by improved leadership and training, returning others to duty. Further, the Army is using greater selectivity in the procurement of new personnel.

The outstanding recent change in punitive-discharge releases occurred in the restoration field. The restoration percentage of all releases tripled during January–June 1959, as compared to 1958—an increase from 8 to 24 percent of all releases. Almost half of these restorations followed the United States Court of Military Appeals decisions (United States vs. May, 10 USCMA 358, 27 CMR 432, and United States vs. Cecil,

10 USCMA 371, 27 CMR 445) which held that a prisoner whose punitive discharge had been suspended must be restored to duty upon his release from confinement unless the suspension is vacated by reason of the prisoner's misconduct subsequent to suspension action. Theretofore, most of these discharges were executed even though clemency was granted in the form of sentence reduction or parole. But even excluding these, the percent otherwise restored (12.9) was substantially more than the 1958 percentage of 7.7 of all releases.

These figures summarize the prisoner movement and clemency, restoration, and parole actions for the period 1 July 1955–30 June 1959:

General Courts-Martial	19,479
Total Punitive-Discharge Confinements	15,913
Punitive-Discharge Confinements to Disciplinary Barracks	12,145
Restoration to Duty of Punitive-Discharge Prisoners	1,324
Clemency Actions in Cases of Prisoners in Disciplinary Barracks and Federal Institutions	3,360
Parole Approvals: Prisoners in Disciplinary Barracks	2,695

The overall program of confinement, correction, rehabilitation, granting of clemency and parole, and restoration to duty of military prisoners is an important and integral part of the Army mission. The Army was not fully organized or essentially equipped for this mission at the beginning of World War II, but during the war it expended every effort to improve and adapt its policies and procedures to cope with a rapidly increasing and then rapidly decreasing prisoner population. Later, the Army drew extensively on its World War II experience to devise the best possible prisoner program which would be adaptable for use in war and peace.

The program for punitive-discharge prisoners in disciplinary barracks, rehabilitation centers (only operated in times of emergency), and Federal institutions has emphasized centralization and uniformity of treatment. Prior to 1946, all confinement operations, including stockades, were under the control of the

Adjutant General. They have since been transferred to the Provost Marshal General's supervision, and today all correctional activities are centralized in this office.

Agreements were worked out with the Department of the Air Force, the Department of the Navy, the Federal Bureau of Prisons of the Department of Justice, and the Federal Probation Service of the United States Courts. A Joint Army and Air Force Clemency and Parole Board was established at departmental level in 1949 to provide centralized and uniform consideration of prisoners for clemency and parole. Authority to grant restoration to duty in the cases of all punitive-discharge prisoners except those in local stockades was also centralized at departmental level, but it is separate from the clemency and parole functions.

Evaluation of Current Program

The data presented up to this point tend to emphasize the importance of restoration as a vital part of the Army's correction program; however, the primary purpose of *this* study is to evaluate the effectiveness of the current procedure for selecting candidates for restoration to duty. What happens to individuals who are restored to honorable duty status? Do they become effective soldiers or do they revert to their previous pattern of behavior unacceptable to the Army? An examination of the records of those restored to duty should assist us to evaluate our procedures.

In January 1958, the Office of the Provost Marshal General began to list chronologically those Army prisoners restored to honorable duty status by Department of the Army action. This date, therefore, was selected as the starting point of a survey to measure adjustment to military life of individuals restored to duty. To provide maximum utility the data should be as current as possible, yet sufficient time must have been spent on active duty following restoration to measure adjustment in terms of probable permanence. The date selected, which best met both of these conditions, was 1 June 1964. Records revealed that during the period between these two dates, 1 January 1958 and

1 June 1964, the Army restored 805 punitive-discharge prisoners to duty. A search of the personnel files of the Office of the Adjutant General, Department of the Army, revealed that 434 of these 805 individuals had subsequently been discharged from the Army.

Some indication of the success or failure of the restoration program might be gained by determining the conditions under which these 434 restorees were discharged. As a result of a search of retired records by personnel of the U.S. Army Records Center, St. Louis, Missouri, it was revealed that 308 or 71 percent of the discharged restorees had been discharged under honorable conditions and that 126 or 29 percent had been discharged under less than honorable conditions. Based on these figures, the effectiveness of the restoration procedures for that group no longer in the active establishment would appear to be 71 percent successful.

Of primary concern to the Army, however, is not the group which has already been discharged, but rather, the individuals restored to duty who remain in an active status. What has happened to the 371 restorees who remain in the active establishment? Are they effective soldiers, and have they proven worthy of the second chance given to them by the Army's restoration program?

In an attempt to answer these and related questions a form was devised which attempted to measure adjustment to military life. To prepare a report form which accurately reflects human behavior and effectiveness is at best a very difficult task. The many types of grading systems used in public school systems over the years to measure academic progress and even closer to home, the variety of efficiency reports used by the Army to measure past effectiveness and future potential bear mute witness to the difficulty of the problem. The problem of evaluating the success of a restoree is more difficult by reason of the fact that the man involved has been given the opportunity to rectify his past errors and must not be made to feel that he is under constant surveillance. Despite the difficulty of the problem, however, tools useful to management which accurately reflect past progress and probable future potential are required and must be devised despite the difficulty involved and their recognized shortcomings. The form developed for use in this study to measure adjustment to military life of the restoree falls in this same category; a useful management tool that reflects the views of the individual who completes the form, at the time that he completes it. There are dangers in using regular administrative channels to obtain information as to the adjustment of a former prisoner. To prevent a stigma from being attached to the man by making known his former status to his peer group and immediate supervisor, a subterfuge was employed and the survey was administered as an "Enlisted Personnel Record Review." A Department of the Army letter was dispatched to the immediate commanding officers of record of each of the 371 restorees reported to be in the active service, requesting completion of the form and a personal evaluation of the restoree assigned to his unit. The data presented below represents the results of this survey.

Unit Commander Evaluation of Army Restorees

Of the 371 letters dispatched to unit commanders, requesting evaluation of the overall efficiency and conduct of the restoree assigned to his unit, replies containing completed Enlisted Personnel Record Review forms were received from 314. Additional communications to the effect that the restoree in question had been discharged were received from 21 commanders. Thus the total response to the survey was 335 replies or 90 percent of the potential of 371. Of the 21 discharged, 15 or 71 percent were discharged under honorable conditions and 6 or 29 percent were discharged under conditions less than honorable. This percentage is identical to that for the group reported to be discharged prior to dispatch of surveys to unit commanders. All of the tables presented in this section are based on the 314 completed record review forms returned by the restoree's unit commanders.

The unit commanders noted the overall usefulness of restorees to the organization and the United States Army. A significant determination from this data is that restorees rate exceedingly high when compared with other soldiers by their immediate unit commanders. Eighty-three percent (83%) ranked in the top half of the rating scale, whereas only 17 percent were in the lower half. Even more significant is the finding that more than 40 percent of the restorees were ranked by their commanders in either the first or second position.

The unit commanders' current ratings of restorees on conduct and efficiency included such factors as work skill, initiative, cooperation, reliability, physical condition, potential, conduct, leadership capacity, and ability to carry out work assignments efficiently and effectively. The resultant ratings may be given in the following percentages: on conduct, 77.7 of the restorees rated excellent; 8.9, good; 6.7, fair; and 6.7, unsatisfactory. The efficiency ratings were 78.7, excellent; 7.9, good; 8.6, fair; and 4.8, unsatisfactory. Worthy of note is the fact that more than 75 percent of all restorees were top rated by their commanders in Conduct and Efficiency.

Two additional types of data were gathered in this survey in an attempt to determine more precisely the *degree* of adjustment of restorees. These indications include number of promotions and demotions earned and the current rank of the restoree; the hypothesis is that these factors are correlates of degree of success.

The data in Table 5 show that since being returned to

5. Promotions and Demotions of Restorees

Number Received by Restorees	Promotions		Demotions	
	Number	Percent	Number	Percent
0	50	15.9	282	90.0
1	123	39.2	26	8.3
2	55	17.5	5	1.6
3	53	16.9	1	.1
4 or more	33	10.5	—	—
Totals	314	100.0	314	100.0

duty, 84.1 percent of all restorees have been promoted one or more times and that over 90 percent have not been demoted.

This would tend to indicate that over 80 percent of the group have made a successful adjustment to military life. Since there are many factors which enter into the promotion of an individual, the 15.9 percent who have failed to be promoted even once cannot necessarily be called failures; the 10 percent who have been demoted have failed to make the proper adjustment however, in that demotions are only made for cause.

A further indication of the degree of adjustment of the restorees is the grade level of the restoree at the time of the report. The lowest ranks of E-1 or E-2 were held by 9.3 percent of the restorees; E-3 by 28.6 percent; E-4 by 25.5 percent; E-5 by 25.2 percent; and E-6 or above by 11.4 percent. Perhaps the most significant findings here is that over 60 percent of the restorees hold permanent appointments in grade E-4 or above. Position vacancies are not required for promotion to E-3 and below, but to be promoted to E-4 and above the restoree must compete with all eligible enlisted men in the unit for the appointment. Considering that most restorees return to duty in the grade of Pvt. E-2, the fact that 90.7 percent currently hold the grade of PFC E-3 or higher, indicates a relatively high rate of rank improvement.

SUMMARY

The data presented in this section tends to show that unit commanders rate their restorees rather highly. In addition to the data presented in tabular form, 126 or 40 percent of the unit commanders expressed laudatory comments concerning their restorees or reported that letters of appreciation and/or letters of commendation had been awarded to them. Typical of the expressions received are the following:

This man is one of the best NCO's I have ever seen. He knows his duty and does it without waiting for instructions.

An exceptionally hard working and conscientious individual who is the most knowledgeable EM I have ever known in his grade and position.

His conduct is above reproach. For outstanding work under adverse conditions he was promoted to E-5 in this unit.

An exceptionally competent Supply Sergeant.

A truly outstanding noncommissioned officer who performs all tasks with enthusiasm.

This NCO is outstanding in all respects. His performance of duty, sense of responsibility, and attitude are exemplary.

Highly respected by his superiors as well as his subordinates. His military bearing, manner of personal performance, personal appearance, and technical knowledge as an Engineer Missile Equipment specialist are all superior.

He has displayed an initiative and efficiency seldom encountered.

An excellent example of a man who has rehabilitated himself through his own determination. He is an asset to his unit and to the Service.

His performance of duty as Platoon Sergeant and his character could not be rated anything but outstanding.

Has demonstrated great potential as an air traffic controller and as operations NCO. A definite asset to this unit and to the Army.

The above comments are by no means unique and could be found in nearly any group of efficiency reports on personnel in a typical effective Army unit. When considered in the light that they were made concerning individuals who were adjudged failures and had been discharged from the Army under less than honorable service, they take on a new perspective and speak well of the Army as an important rehabilitative instrument of American society. As in all studies regarding human behavior, all individuals have not measured up to the potential expected of them. Forty-seven or 15 percent of the study group were subject to some form of disciplinary action, or were the target of unflattering remarks by their unit commander.

The Army does not attempt to label as a Success or as a Failure each individual who participates in the Restoration Program. It is very difficult, therefore, to categorically evaluate our efforts in this area. From the tabular and narrative data presented in this section we have attempted to present an evaluation, by his commanding officer, of each individual restored to duty. From these data it would appear, in summary, that 83 percent are ranked in the top half of a rating scale which attempts to measure the individual's worth to his unit and to the Army; in the areas of conduct and efficiency, 77.7 percent were rated as Excellent in Conduct and 78.7 percent as Excellent in Efficiency; 84.1 percent have been promoted, at least once, and 62 percent hold permanent appointments in grade E-4, or higher, after having commenced their postrestoration active service, for the most part, in grade E-2.

We will attempt at this time to make these figures more meaningful, by comparing them, subject to the availability of a comparable statistical base, with some other agencies which attempt to bring about changes in human behavior to an acceptable social norm.

Restoration of Air Force Prisoners

The United States Air Force operates a specialized prisoner retraining center, the 320th Retraining Group, with the primary mission of restoring to duty Air Force prisoners confined as a result of court-martial. Following conviction by court-martial, Air Force prisoners who have received sentences to confinement are confined by the commander exercising general court-martial jurisdiction, as follows: *1]* those with short sentences and those recommended to be administratively discharged are confined in local stockades; *2]* those considered to be potentially restorable are sent to the 320th Retraining Group (hereinafter referred to as RTG), and *3]* those convicted of serious offenses and not initially considered to be restorable, are sent to the United States Disciplinary Barracks, Fort Leavenworth, Kansas. Since 1952, approximately seven thousand prisoners have been processed through the RTG and approximately 50 percent have been returned to duty. The statistics used in this section all refer to Airmen returned to duty from the RTG and it is important to remember that this is a select group consisting of those considered to have a high potential for restoration.

The data in Table 6 are based on questionnaires completed by squadron commanders on all restorees and afford a direct comparison with the Army restoree data. The data cover a five and one-half-year period from 1 July 1955 through 31 December

1960, whereas the Army data cover a five and one-half-year period from 1 January 1958 through 30 June 1964. It should be noted that the Air Force rating scale is in reverse order to that of the Army in that an Air Force rating of 1 is Worst, whereas an Army rating 1 is Best. Squadron commanders rated 58.6 percent of their restorees in the upper half of the scale, as compared to 83 percent for the Army.

6. Commander Ratings of Restorees on Usefulness to Organization and Air Force or Army

Air Force				Army		
Scale	Number	Percent		Scale	Number	Percent
1 (Worst)	117	11.1		10 (Worst)	14	4.5
2	46	4.4		9	5	1.6
3	53	5.0		8	16	5.1
4	81	7.7		7	8	2.5
5	139	13.2		6	11	3.5
6	178	16.8		5	31	9.8
7	168	15.8		4	45	14.4
8	140	13.2		3	50	15.9
9	63	6.0		2	70	22.3
10 (Best)	72	6.8		1 (Best)	64	20.4
Total	1057	100.0			314	100.0

Squadron Commanders' ratings of performance of duty over the three-year period covering 1958 through 1960 included such factors as work skill, initiative, cooperation, study for work improvement, leadership capacity, and ability to carry out work assignments efficiently and effectively. Of 456 restorees, 32.2 percent were rated above average; 49.1 percent, average; and 18.7 percent, below average. These ratings, although not identical, can be related to the Army restoree ratings. Army Unit Commanders rated over 75 percent of their restorees as excellent in Conduct and Efficiency as compared to 32.2 percent in the above average category for the Airman restoree.

Over a three-year base period of 1958–60, only 2 percent

of all Airman restorees had reached grade E-4 or higher six months after restoration. E-3 levels were attained by 9.6 percent, E-2 by 65.4 percent, and E-1 by 23.0 percent of these restorees. It was noted earlier that 62 percent of the Army restorees attained the grade of E-4 or higher. These statistics are not exactly comparable since the Army data showed the *current* grade level attained *six months after restoration.*

The Air Force attempts to evaluate the outcome of their correctional program by presenting quantitative data which considers success from three standpoints: short-term success, total short-term success rate, and long-term success. Since "short-term" in this incidence refers to restorees who continue to serve in the Air Force in an acceptable manner six months after being returned to duty from the Retraining Group and those few who may have been discharged during their time under honorable conditions, "long-term" success more closely parallels the evaluation of the Army restoree as considered in this study. "Long-term" success is defined as including restorees who performed satisfactorily in the Air Force to the completion of their current enlistment, and who have either received a discharge under honorable conditions or have been permitted to reenlist. Even this definition does not exactly describe the Army restoree of this study, in that many of the earlier restorees have reenlisted

7. *Air Force Long-Term Success-Failure Rates, 1952–60*

Year	Total Number Restored	Success		Failure	
		Number	Percent	Number	Percent
1952	302	172	57.0	130	43.0
1953	307	201	65.5	106	34.5
1954	321	224	69.8	97	30.2
1955	416	283	68.0	133	32.0
1956	262	180	68.7	82	31.3
1957	254	157	61.8	97	38.2
1958	333	198	59.5	135	40.5
1959	252	181	71.8	71	28.2
1960	218	185	84.9	33	15.1

during the five and one-half-year span of the study yet are still considered to be restorees by the Army. The data in Table 7 show the long-term success-failure rates of the Retraining Group for each year for the period 1952–60. It should be noted that the 1960 success rate is artificially high, since many of the restorees returned to duty during 1960 were still serving current enlistments at the time the data were collected (January–June 1961) and some may fail before completing their enlistment period.

Restoration of Naval Prisoners

Since the Naval Retraining Command compares more nearly to the United States Army Disciplinary Barracks than does the Air Force Prisoner Retraining Group (RTG), a study was made of available statistics on Navy prisoners restored to duty (Department of the Navy, 1959–62). Again, the statistical base is quite different in that the Navy reports on *all* prisoners returned to duty after serving a period of confinement in a Naval Retraining Command and not just those who are restored to duty after having been awarded a punitive type discharge. The Navy studies reports on the performance of prisoners after they had served a six-month probationary period following restoration to duty and after having served a period of confinement in a Naval Retraining Command. Statistics were available for a three and one-half-year period, starting 1 January 1958 (the same date as the beginning of the Army study) and terminating 30 June 1961. The Navy reports as a success, restorees who are on active duty six months following restoration with no further offenses, those separated under "favorable" conditions, and those on active duty with lost time totaling less than fifteen days. Reported as failures are those on active duty with time lost totaling fifteen days or more, "unfavorable" separations, and those with punitive discharges. A "favorable" discharge is awarded to those who have a clear conduct record after restoration. As far as the Navy is concerned, a man with a clear conduct record who is administratively discharged or relieved from active duty is a success. If he has additional offenses on record after restoration and is then administratively separated, he is a failure.

The "number" shown on Table 8 indicates the actual number of Naval prisoners returned to duty status on whom reports are available. This number is considerably larger than that for the Army because Army figures are limited to restorees with punitive discharges restored to duty by Department of the Army action. Using their own criteria for evaluating performance, the Navy reports 62.8 percent success of the restoration aspect of the disciplinary command program.

8. Performance Study of Navy Prisoners Restored to Duty, Jan. 1958–June 1961

Period	Total Number Restored	Success		Failure	
		Number	Percent	Number	Percent
1 Jan. 1958–30 June 1958	1539	970	63.0	569	37.0
1 July 1958–31 Dec. 1958	1539	970	63.0	569	37.0
1 Jan. 1959–30 June 1959	1013	634	62.6	379	37.4
1 July 1959–31 Dec. 1959	1013	634	62.6	379	37.4
1 Jan. 1960–30 June 1960	652	396	60.7	256	39.3
1 July 1960–31 Dec. 1960	173	116	67.0	57	33.0
1 Jan. 1961–30 June 1961	47	32	68.0	15	32.0
Total	5976	3752	62.8	2224	37.2

Comparison with Civilian Programs

Because of the wide variation that exists between correctional institutions in the United States in methods of operation and goals, the criteria to measure adjustment success, and in follow-up procedures, comparative analysis is exceedingly difficult. However, some rough comparisons are possible.

Considering all types of prisoners in civilian penal institutions, the group which bears the closest similarity to the Army restoree is the parolee from state and federal correctional institutions. For the most part, both groups of individuals have made the best use of treatment facilities available while in confinement and show the most potential of adjustment to the freedom of the open community. Trained correctional experts have evaluated each individual from an adjustment standpoint and have made judgments changing the custody classification of both the parolee and restoree from that of a prisoner behind bars to that of an individual in a free community. Both groups are subject to supervision, and are required to measure up to certain standards in order to succeed.

In viewing the results of several long-term parole studies, Tappan (1960) reports as follows: *1]* New York State—56.8 parole success among parolees of the state institution over the period 1953–58; *2]* California—49.1 percent parole success among parolees of state institutions over the period 1947–50; and *3]* New Jersey—59.5 percent parole success among parolees of the state institution over the period 1948–53. These states are considered to have the most effective parole system in the United States and should, therefore, afford the most valid measurement against which comparison with the Army Restoration Program might be made.

Based upon figures obtained from Mr. Louis Sharpe, Chief of Probation of the Federal Probation System, during a recent course of instruction at the American University, Washington, D.C., approximately 73 percent of those prisoners granted parole by the United States Board of Parole, successfully complete their period of supervision, and 27 percent fail and are returned to the institution from which they were released. This Federal success rate is considerably higher than that reported for the states above, but it is not dissimilar to the 71 percent figure previously reported for restorees discharged from the Army under honorable conditions.

The disparity between the success rate of the states as compared to that of the Federal system supports the contention that the state of correctional follow-up statistics is such that comparison should be made only with extreme caution. This does not negate, however, the usefulness of such comparison.

Major Findings and Conclusions

The United States Army operated during World War II the largest correctional and confinement system ever operated in the United States of America.

The Army's World War II restoration program was a tremendous achievement in that 42,000 of the 84,000 prisoners sentenced to punitive type discharges were restored to honorable duty.

Between January 1958 and June 1964 the Army restored to honorable duty status by Department of the Army action 805 prisoners sentenced to punitive type discharges. Of this number, 434 were discharged prior to the initiation of this study. Discharged under honorable conditions were 308 or 71 percent; under less than honorable conditions, 126 or 29 percent.

The group still in the active service are rated by their immediate unit commander as follows:

Usefulness to Organization and the Army:	83% in top half of rating scale.
Conduct & Efficiency:	75% rated Excellent.
Promotions earned:	84% promoted at least once.
	10% demoted.
Current grade level:	62% in grade E-4 or higher.

From the figures shown above, it would appear that 71 percent of the restorees no longer in the Army succeeded, and that about 75 percent of those still on active duty are progressing satisfactorily.

Air Force Unit commanders rate their restorees as follows:

Usefulness to Organization and Air Force:	59% in top half of rating scale.
Conduct and Efficiency:	32% above average
Current grade level:	2% in grade E-4 or higher

Air Force statistics report a long-term success rate of 66.8 percent.

The Navy reports 62.8 percent success of the restoration aspect of the disciplinary command programs.

The Federal Probation System reports that approximately 73 percent of those prisoners granted parole by the United States Board of Parole successfully complete this period of supervision.

The differing success rates must be interpreted with caution since success criteria and time samplings in follow-up inquiries were variable.

III

RESEARCH APPROACHES

10

Role Perceptions in the Military Prison

NORMAN E. EGGLESTON

In total institutions, such as prisons, roles are assigned and only to a limited extent can the individual affect the way his role is defined. It is not what he brings to the setting which determines how others will react to him, and what they will expect of him, but largely the nature of the role to which he is assigned (Zald, 1960).

There is considerable agreement in the literature of penology that the social roles of staff, guards, and inmates are prescribed by the prison culture more comprehensively and stringently than in any noninstitutional milieu. "The number of roles an individual may play are severely limited and, once assigned, are maintained—particularly at the lower-status levels —with enormous group pressures. The degree to which the individual can partake in the selection of his role is similarly limited and conditional" (McCorkle and Korn, 1962).

There is some evidence that roles are perceived differently in institutions which have a therapeutic orientation. Street (1965) studied inmates' role perceptions in juvenile correctional institutions and found that inmates in such a setting more often expressed positive attitudes toward the staff, revealed less evidence of prisonization on the "solidary opposition" model, and demonstrated positive evidence of self-change.

Role perceptions very much determine behavior and attitudes in social relationships. As Perlman (1961) writes, "Social roles mark out what a person in a given social position and situation is expected to be, to act like, and to feel like. . . . Our actions are heavily determined by our ideas of role requirements and expectations."

The present research explored the role perceptions of inmates, custodial staff, and treatment staff in a correctional setting. It explored the conditions assumed necessary by treatment staff for therapeutic relationships with inmates. This involved such questions as how the inmates perceive guards and treatment staff, whether the inmates accept a complementary client role or that of hostile opposition, and the relationships between guards and staff. The operational measures used in this study were the perceptions of role expectations and the degree to which role expectations and role performances coincided.

Hypotheses and Method

Four null hypotheses were developed regarding the nature of role perceptions in the institution. The first two were general hypotheses and the remaining two were derived from these.

1] Ratings of the roles of guard, staff, and prisoners are distributed randomly. This is a basic question which deals with the existence of role differentiation: Do subjects describe the three roles differently?

2] The role of the sources does not affect role perceptions. This is the complementary question to the first hypotheses: Are the perceptions by subjects within a role different from those sources in another role?

3] Military rank does not influence role perceptions. This hypothesis is of importance because of the difference in amount of contact of high- and low-ranking guards and staff with the prisoners, and also because of the influence on policy of the higher-ranking guards and staff.

4] Length of stay does not affect role perceptions. This hypothesis is of particular importance for the inmates, for it explores whether there is change in perceptions during confinement.

A role performance questionnaire was developed from Jourard's work (1957) on self-evaluation. Factor analysis of the instrument has suggested high loadings for social desirability for male subjects. The questionnaire required the subjects to rate ideal and actual roles of guards, staff, and prisoners on forty paired descriptions of attitudes, traits, and behavior. Socially desirable characteristics included such ratings as "good sense of humor," "even-tempered," "can express self very readily." A five point scale was used to score the responses. The forty items were the same as those used in non-prison settings and therefore were intended to reflect desirable social norms for any general population.

Some of the items as they appeared on the instrument were as follows:

	guards	
	actual	ideal
1] humorless 1 2 3 4 5 good sense of humor	———	———
2] very intelligent 1 2 3 4 5 stupid	———	———

PROCEDURE

All research was done at the United States Disciplinary Barracks, Fort Leavenworth, Kansas. The population was young, there were many prisoners who had no punitive discharge from the Army and were to return to active duty, and there was little pessimism about the possibility of rehabilitation for at least some of the population. The sources of the ratings was composed of approximately a third of the individuals in each of the major roles in the institution. There were 160 prisoners sampled from approximately seven hundred inmates in the population. There were 133 guards of approximately four hundred assigned. And there were 89 staff members in the sample representing about two hundred staff other than those assigned primarily to Directorate of Custody. There were 382 subjects in the total sample.

The research design basically consisted of having each subject make six ratings for each item; three were of the ways guards, staff, and prisoners ought to be (ideal) and three of the ways they were (actual). The guard subjects were subdivided into high-ranking (E-5 and above), low-ranking (below E-5) and new guards. Staff were subdivided by rank, and prisoners were divided into new (under eight days), short (under a month), medium (four to six months), and long (over a year) subgroups. Each subject in each group rated ideal and actual role performance for each of the three roles on the forty item questionnaire, for a total of 240 ratings elicited per subject.

Results

RATINGS OF INSTITUTIONAL ROLES

The first hypothesis stated that ratings of the roles of guard, staff, and prisoner are distributed randomly. The results rejected this null hypothesis and each role was described differently from the other two. Similarly the second null hypothesis was rejected and significant differences between sources were observed. Table 9, which summarizes the mean ratings for the total groups of 133 guards, 89 staff, and 160 prisoners, shows the pattern of role perceptions which existed.

The role of staff was rated higher than the roles of guard and prisoner for Ideal and Actual ratings. Satisfaction with conformity to role expectations was greatest with the role of staff, as indicated by the low Role Discrepancy scores.

The role of guard was perceived as similar to that of staff by guard and staff raters. Prisoners, however, rated guard Ideal the same as their own Ideal, and they rated the Actual guard role performance almost the same as their own. Guard Role Discrepancy was rated by the prisoners midway between that of the staff and prisoner ratings.

The role satisfaction of prisoner was rated well below that of the other two roles. Staff rated the prisoner Ideal role lower than did the other sources, indicating a lower level of expectation for prisoners than for guards and staff. The guard and prisoner sources agreed on almost identical ratings of the Ideal prisoner role. All source groups agreed on a much lower rating for prisoner's Actual role performance.

Only on the role of staff was there a great deal of agreement by all sources on role expectations, actual role performance, and satisfaction with role performance. The ratings of staff appeared fairly positive; even the prisoners, who tended to make all of their ratings more negative than the others, rated the staff very near to the ratings given them by the other groups.

9. Mean Ratings of Guards, Staff, and Prisoners Role by Guard, Staff, and Prisoner Raters

Group Rated	Source	Mean Ratings		Role Discrepancy[1]
		Ideal	Actual	
	Guard	154	134	42
Guards	Staff	154	127	43
	Prisoner	143	114	58
	Guard	156	134	42
Staff	Staff	159	134	42
	Prisoner	150	128	48
	Guard	144	106	63
Prisoners	Staff	132	108	54
	Prisoner	143	113	64

[1] Role Discrepancy scores were based on the totaled differences between Ideal and Actual on each of the forty items; they were obtained independently of the total Ideal and Actual scores, do not necessarily correspond to the arithmetic Ideal-Actual difference between totals, and probably represent a more sensitive measure of role dissatisfaction.

The Role Discrepancy data and the statistical significances of the differences between the Role Discrepancy ratings and sources are summarized in Table 10. The Critical Ratios (CRs) were calculated for the subjects rated and for the sources. Thus the CR of 6.76 indicates that guards rated staff and prisoners as significantly different in Role Discrepancy; the actual difference between the means was 63 minus 42 or 21. Similarly the CR between guard and staff raters of 2.58 indicates that they were statistically different at the .01 level in perceptions of prisoner Role Discrepancy.

10. Critical Ratios between Role Discrepancy Means of Sources and Subjects Rated

Sources	Means Subjects Rated			Critical Ratios Between Subjects Rated			Critical Ratios Between Sources		
	Guard	Staff	Pris-oner	Guard-Staff	Guard-Pris-oner	Staff-Pris-oner	Guard-Staff	Guard-Pris-oner	Pris-oner-Staff
Staff M	43	40	54	.90	3.46[1]	4.06[1]	.37	.61	2.58[2]
SD	20	23	24						
Prisoner M	58	48	64	3.04[2]	1.70	4.71[1]	6.16[1]	2.14[3]	.09
SD	27	26	26						
Guard M	42	42	63	.00	7.61[1]	6.76[1]	5.18[1]	2.41[3]	2.99[2]

[1] $p < .001$
[2] $p < .01$
[3] $p < .05$

Staff ratings of the guard and staff roles were not significantly different with a CR of .90. However, staff ratings of the roles of guard and prisoner and staff and prisoner were significantly different beyond the .001 level with CRs of 3.46 and 4.06 respectively.

Prisoners perceived guard and staff roles as significantly different, and there were also significant differences in their ratings of staff versus prisoners. Although the prisoners rated guard Role Discrepancy lower than their own, the difference between the two ratings did not attain significance at the .05 level.

From the preceding data it may be noted that the prisoners rated all role performance as more discrepant from ideal expectations than the other raters did. The marked difference from the other ratings was their perception of the role of guard. The prisoners perceived the staff as very different from themselves—in a favorable direction—but they rated the guards as more like prisoners than like staff. Staff did not agree with this prisoner role perception, and the guards emphasized their similarity to staff and their dissimilarity to the prisoner group.

As for the ratings of the role of prisoner, it is the staff which was divergent from the other sources. Staff ratings are relatively favorable for all groups. They perceive themselves as conforming closely to their role expectations. The guards are perceived as performing slightly less adequately. Staff gave a more favorable rating to prisoners than did the guard and prisoner raters.

Each group rated his own role more positively than others rated it. Guards had a particularly equivocal role. Staff agreed with the guards that their ideal role is like that of staff, but prisoners disagreed by rating guards much lower. Guards rated their own actual role performance almost the same as that of staff, while prisoners rated guard's actual role performance nearly the same as role performance of the prisoners.

The between-source correlations for the different roles are presented in Table 11. The correlations between the ratings by guards and staff were very high, ranging from .77 to .89. The remaining correlations were considerably lower, although still positive and significant, and supported the impression that prisoners were least in agreement with other sources.

11. Intercorrelations Among Role Discrepancy Ratings[1]

	Subjects Rated		
Sources Correlated	Staff	Guard	Prisoner
Staff-Guard	.89	.85	.77
Guard-Prisoner	.58	.49	.58
Prisoner-Staff	.39	.48	.47

[1] All correlations differed significantly from chance at the .001 level.

Correlations were calculated between possible combinations of four categories of ratings, Role Discrepancy, Ideal with Actual, Ideal with Ideal, and Actual with Actual, for each of the rater subgroups. Examining the guard ratings first, it was found that on role discrepancy ratings, the index of dissatisfaction, there was a good deal of consistency between the subgroups of guard raters, the new, high-rank, and low-rank guards. Eight of the thirty-six correlations were above $+.82$ and only three were below $+.41$. These generally high correlations indicated that a set pattern operated across the ratings: those who rated one group high tended to rate the others high also, and those who rated one group low tended to rate all groups low.

The guard rating pattern for the Ideal and Actual ratings of the three roles was less clear cut. Except for the new guards, the guards who rated guard ideal high tended also to rate guard actual performance high. For the staff, guards had even a stronger tendency to perceive actual role performance high, if their expectations were high, or low if their expectations were low. For guard ratings of the prisoner role, the opposite results appeared. All of the correlations were significant and negative. Those who had high expectations tended to rate actual performance low, and those with low expectations rated actual performance high. The guards were the only source who demonstrated such a pattern.

Staff sources tended to generalize across roles more than guards, based on the very high correlations obtained. There was also less difference between low-rank and high-rank staff than between the subgroups of guards. Staff ideal and actual expectations were very consistent between the roles. If they rated one high they tended to rate the others high; the correlations were much higher than for the guards.

The prisoner raters were similar to the staff. Correlations tended to be high, and the staff patterns of rating were followed by the prisoners. Role discrepancy ratings were highly correlated, and ideal and actual ratings were quite independent for all ratings. Prisoners who had high expectations for any of the roles tended to have similar high expectations for everyone. Even more than did guard and staff sources, prisoners who perceived actual role performance as high for one group tended to perceive it as high for all groups.

RANK AS A FACTOR IN ROLE PERCEPTIONS

Null hypothesis three stated that military rank does not affect role perceptions. This hypothesis cannot be rejected. None of the Critical Ratios calculated between the means of role discrepancy ratings by high-rank and low-rank staff or high-rank and low-rank guards reached statistical significance at the .05 level.

LENGTH OF STAY AND ROLE PERCEPTIONS

Null hypothesis four stated that length of stay in the institution does not affect role perceptions. The data indicated that this cannot be rejected for guards, but there are differences between prisoner sources of ratings grouped by length of confinement.

The hypothesis was tested by guard and prisoner sources divided by their length of stay. The twenty-five new and sixty-eight low-rank guards were new to the institution. These were compared to forty high-rank guards, nearly all of whom had been assigned for some time. There were forty-three new prisoners who had been confined less than eight days, thirty-three short term prisoners who had been confined about one month, forty-six medium term prisoners whose length of stay was four to six months, and thirty-eight long term prisoners confined over one year.

The test of the tenure hypothesis was to require significant differences between the means of the role discrepancy ratings. No critical ratios for guard sources attained statistical significance. However, there was at least one statistically significant difference in every comparison of prisoner sources, except for ratings of medium-term versus long-term prisoners. The rounded mean scores when guards were rated were new prisoners, forty-nine; short-term prisoners, fifty-two; medium-term prisoners, sixty-four; and long-term prisoners, sixty-seven.

The new and long-term prisoners agreed on the roles of

staff and prisoner, but significantly disagreed on the role of
guard. It was the new prisoners who appeared to enter the institution with expectations most like staff and they perceived guard
roles very differently than did the medium-term and long-term
prisoner. The ratings of the staff and prisoner role improved
for the short-term prisoners, then worsened for the medium-
and long-term prisoners.

Ratings of staff were the most favorable of the three roles
rated for all prisoners, and long-term prisoners rated staff more
positively, with a mean of forty-eight, than did the medium-term
prisoners with a mean of fifty-seven. Only the guard role was
rated worse by each succeeding group of prisoners; the longer
the prisoners were confined the lower the guard was rated.

It appeared that the findings in this section of the study
answered the question of whether prisoners differentiate between guards and staff. The prisoners entered perceiving the
guards and staff as only slightly differentiated, but the longer
they were confined, the more distinction between guards and
staff was seen. Staff was rated fairly positively by all prisoner
groups and only the guard ratings were consistently more negative with longer confinement. In fact, after the initial rating
by the new prisoners, the guard ratings by each group of prisoner raters was almost the same low level as for the prisoner role.

Discussion

This study of role perceptions provided suggestive findings
both in methodology and about the role perceptions of guards,
staff, and inmates in a correctional setting. It appeared that
administration of an instrument such as that used in this study,
which measures the social desirability of role characteristics, can
provide significant measures of institutional role expectations
and behavior, and measures of conformity to role expectations.

The subjects distinguished in their ratings between the
characteristics of guards, staff, and prisoners. Staff were generally
rated most positively, then guards, then prisoners the lowest,
by all rating groups. Guards and staff were perceived to be similar by the guard and staff sources, but prisoners rated guards as

more like prisoners than like staff. Staff expectations were much lower for the role of prisoner than were guard and prisoner expectations.

Guards are in an awkward position based on the results observed. They view themselves as similar to staff, but staff rate their own role higher than the guard role, and prisoners rate guards like prisoners, not like staff. Thus guards find themselves defined as lower in status.

Regardless of the problems which lack of agreement on the characteristics of the roles might create, it is clear that the conditions for treatment in the institution are satisfied. There is differentiation by the prisoners between the guard and staff role. The guard role is perceived as less positive than staff and seems to indicate identification of the prisoner with the guard, with the implication that the guard is really no different from prisoners. This may be a positive view, in one sense, for it could indicate the prisoners feel capable of returning to the role of guard—or low-ranking soldier—with comparative ease. And finally, we find that the prisoners perceive themselves as expected to perform at a fairly positive level, the same as they expect of guards and not much lower than they expect of staff, and concurrently view themselves as performing considerably below their expected level.

The finding that the prisoners perceived the role of staff as a positive one fits the social purpose of staff as a role model of desirable behavior. The negative finding similar to this was the prisoner's perception of guards becoming more and more negative with increased length of stay in the institution. This would indicate that the prisoner who established a positive relationship with a staff member would be unlikely to find a great deal of opposition from other prisoners. However, the prisoner who did not develop over time the negative conception of the guard could be regarded as differing distinctly from his peers.

It was noted that high-rank guards were much like the low-rank staff in their perceptions of guards and staff. Low-rank guards were relatively critical of guard and staff roles and extremely critical of prisoner nonconformity to role expectations. It appeared that the high-rank guards had not been able to pass on their relaxed perceptions of expectations of prisoners, while the high-rank staff were unrealistically different in their expectations from other guards and staff.

Low-rank guards were among the most demanding of all the institutional groups in their perceptions of how prisoners should perform, and were in a position to observe the prisoner behaving less adequately than expected. Considerable tension between the low-rank guards and the prisoners would be anticipated. This possibility increased with the finding that the prisoners develop more negative attitudes toward the guards as they remain in the Disciplinary Barracks longer. This mutual antagonism is predictive of chronic tension. Since the high-rank guards and particularly high-rank staff do not share the guard's evaluation of the situation, the guard is likely to find himself repeatedly defined as too demanding when he reports misbehavior. This may account for frequent feelings of the guard that he is compromising his standards if he does not take disciplinary action, or that he must tend toward exaggerating the seriousness of the offense he does report in order to insure that the prisoner is punished.

Steady progression of more unfavorable prisoner attitudes toward guards over time was observed. The findings indicated that the prisoners were prepared to view guards as similar to staff when they arrive. But the longer they remain the more sharply the prisoners distinguish between the staff, who are rated positively, and the guards, who are rated as like the prisoners.

Perceptions of Staff by prisoners of varying tenure formed a puzzling pattern. Ratings of Staff Role Discrepancy began at forty-four by the new Prisoner, went down to forty by the short-term Prisoner, jumped markedly to fifty-seven in ratings by the medium-term Prisoner, then went back down to forty-eight by the long-term Prisoner.

One clue to this oscillation is that the ratings of their own role by the prisoner follows a similar pattern. A second is the proposition that prisoners at the beginning and end of their terms reflect "outside" values more, while those in the middle of their sentence tend to reflect prisoner norms of institutional behavior. A third is the pattern of Staff contact with the prisoners, which involves extensive evaluation shortly after admission, the period the short-term Prisoners were in, and less contact thereafter except on an individual basis. A fourth factor is the pattern of giving favorable custody and work assignments to Prisoners who have been in the Disciplinary Barracks for a time without any major trouble.

Putting these together, we would hazard that increased contact with Staff and longer term acquaintance with Staff, particularly when institutional rewards have resulted, lead to more favorable role perceptions. Less contact with Staff coupled with few institutional rewards, leads to generally hostile reactions.

One finding which was surprising in its consistency was the Prisoner perception of the role of Prisoner. One might expect bravado, projection, and denial, resulting in favorable ratings of the role of Prisoner. The actual findings were that Prisoners and other sources rated the Prisoner Ideal role the lowest, the Actual role performance the lowest, and the Role Discrepancy the greatest.

Among the conditions for a therapeutic relationship must be evidence that the treatment person is able to deal effectively with his role, and the client's self-perception that he fails to conform to his expectations in role performance. The role discrepancy ratings by the prisoners in this study indicate a potential for therapeutic relationships. Prisoners defined the staff role as conforming closely to role expectations and their own role as falling significantly below expected performance. Prisoners' descriptions of the role of guard were relatively favorable in the early stages of the prisoner's confinement, became more negative with longer stay, but never became more negative than their own role performance evaluations.

Staff rated the ideal Prisoner role much lower than did Guard or Prisoner raters, who rated it almost identically. This appears to reflect an attitude of decreasing expectations to a level of performance which the Prisoners can attain more easily, rather than a philosophy of expecting Prisoners to learn to conform to a considerably higher level of social norms. Such a conflict in philosophy, with Staff holding to modest improvement in behavior, may account for some of the custody-treatment conflict which is so often documented in the literature of penology.

Summary

This study investigated ideal, actual, and discrepant role perceptions of guards, staff, and inmates in a military correctional setting. The subjects were 160 prisoners, 133 guards, and 89 staff, or approximately a third of those assigned to or confined in the institution. A 40 item questionnaire was administered in which all of the subjects made ratings of the way guards, staff, and prisoners actually were and ought to be. The hypotheses dealt with the nature of the roles, the influence of group membership on role perceptions, and the influence of rank and length of stay in the institution of role perceptions.

The staff role was rated positively, the guard role was rated like the staff role by guards and staff but like the prisoner role by prisoners, and the prisoner role was rated as conforming poorly to expectations. Each group tended to rate itself more positively than it was rated by the other two groups. There were significant differences for inmates of varying length of confinement. The longer inmates stayed, the more negative their perceptions of guards. This contrasted with guard ratings, which became more positive with longer stay in the setting.

There were no roles in the institution which were free of ambiguity. Each group—guard, staff member, or prisoner—was in substantial disagreement with another group about their perceptions of another role. Guards and staff disagreed about prisoners. Prisoners and staff, and prisoners and guards disagreed about guards. Thus since role expectations were not clear for all participants, the institution in which this research was done must anticipate organizational misperceptions. The conditions for treatment were seen as possible in this military correctional institution since the roles of staff and prisoner included desirable role models and motivation for prisoner change.

11

Mental Disease and Ability in Military Prisoners

STANLEY L. BRODSKY

Mental Disease

The identification of selected criminals as insane has moved from the Wild Beast Test of 1723, in which insanity was defined as cognitive functioning at the level of a newborn infant or wild beast, to the Durham Rule, which defined legal insanity as the product of substantial mental disease or defect, and has reflected an increasing broad legal view of insanity. Concomitant with this trend a great deal of attention has been attracted to the psychological state of criminals during confinement, and indeed, psychiatric evaluation in confinement may represent a kind of laboratory test for the efficiency of the court system of screening out the insane.

The observation has been frequently made that there are many disturbed individuals imprisoned, although it has also been noted that "the number of schizophrenic prison inmates has never been accurately established" (Bluestone and Perkins, 1965). Thurrell, Halleck, and Johnsen (1965) have pointed out that 15 percent of the Wisconsin prison population in 1958 had a history of prior mental hospitalization. A rare positive report has appeared in the New York State ratings of 57.5 percent of over seven thousand inmates released during 1963 as having "mature and normal" attitudes toward other inmates (State of New York, Department of Correction, 1963).

The evaluation method used at the U.S. Disciplinary Barracks for estimation of presence and type of mental disease represents a rather direct transfer of the mental hospital model. All entering prisoners are seen by a member of the social-work staff for a social history, are administered group psychological tests, presently Minnesota Multiphasic Personality Inventories (MMPI) and Sentence Completion Tests, and are seen by a psychiatrist for an interview leading to a psychiatric diagnosis and recommendations regarding restoration to military duty, clemency, parole, job, and level of custody. Related information is elicited from prisoner relatives, former military units, home police authorities, and the FBI.

The psychiatric diagnoses of all prisoners from fiscal year 1942 through 1966 are shown in Table 12. The primary findings were that about four-fifths of the prisoners were diagnosed as character and behavior disorders and about one-fifth as having no psychiatric disease. Considerable variability was present overall and particularly in the period from 1942 to 1955. From 1944 to the present at least two-thirds of the population were diagnosed as having a character or behavior disorder, with the range during this period extending from 66.7 to 94.4 percent. Over 50 percent were identified as having no psychiatric disorder in 1942 and 1943; following that time interval, the range varied from 1.6 percent in 1950 to 30.4 percent in 1959. The marked discrepancy between the first two years of the reported data and the remaining ones may well have been due to real differences in prisoner personality features as much as diagnostic inconsistency, for it was noted in the 1943 U.S. Disciplinary Barracks Annual Report by the Division of Psychiatry and Sociology that "Since the new regulations with respect to the types of offenders to be committed to this institution went into effect on 1 Dec. 42, the quality of the inmates committed here has shown a decided decline."

A low incidence of diagnosed psychoneurotic and psychotic disorders was present. None were reported in several years and the maximum percents were 2.4 and 3.2 for psychoneurosis and psychosis, respectively. The group of miscellaneous diagnoses for the most part represented less than 4 percent of the subjects, although in 1952 and 1953 it rose to 8.4 and 11.2 percent. This rise was the result of a large proportion of prisoners being diagnosed as having "disorders of intelligence."

The consistency was quite high over the last seven years of reporting, from 1960 through 1966. There was less than two

12. Psychiatric Diagnoses of the Inmate Population in the USDB from July 1941 through June 1966, by Fiscal Year

			Percent			
Year[1]	Total Number Examined	No Psychiatric Disorders	Character and Behavior Disorders	Psychoneurosis	Psychosis	Miscellaneous
1942	502	52.8	41.6	0.0	0.8	4.8
1943	2312	51.2	46.0	0.3	0.2	2.3
1944	1841	21.9	74.9	1.4	0.2	1.8
1945	1750	17.5	78.7	1.0	0.5	2.2
1946	844	19.9	71.9	0.1	1.7	6.4
1947	[2]	[2]	[2]	[2]	[2]	[2]
1948	[2]	[2]	[2]	[2]	[2]	[2]
1949	1435	8.1	87.5	0.0	0.9	3.5
1950	942	1.6	94.4	0.7	2.0	1.3
1951	1381	28.2	66.7	1.7	2.1	1.4
1952	1712	18.6	67.4	2.3	3.2	8.4
1953	1458	14.3	70.3	1.7	2.5	11.2
1954	1137	8.4	86.8	2.0	2.0	0.7
1955	2043	6.5	90.6	2.4	0.2	0.3
1956	1626	22.1	74.1	0.7	2.3	0.7
1957	1464	13.8	83.5	1.2	1.4	0.1
1958	2053	22.0	76.8	0.3	0.6	0.3
1959	1443	30.4	68.7	0.3	0.4	0.3
1960	1830	22.6	75.7	1.0	0.5	0.2
1961	1103	22.4	75.1	1.1	0.4	1.0
1962	1081	23.3	74.7	0.9	0.0	1.1
1963	1154	22.4	74.3	0.1	0.0	3.2
1964	1212	16.9	80.2	0.0	0.0	2.9
1965	1143	23.3	75.4	0.1	0.5	0.7
1966	1045	22.5	74.3	1.2	0.5	1.5

[1] Data for 1942–58 were excerpted from a report by Richard A. Cook titled "Psychiatric Assessment of Military Offenders" and presented to the Third Annual Conference of U.S. Army Clinical Psychologists, Chicago, Illinois, 31 August 1960.
[2] Not reported.

percentage points variation in the diagnostic categories of no disorder and character and behavior disorder among six of the seven years. The consistency over time represents a substantial reliability in ratings, in contrast to other methods of study of psychiatric diagnostic reliability (Ash, 1949; Stoller and Geerstma, 1963). However at a given point in time it has been found that much inter-psychiatrist variability is present in this military setting. Cook (1960) compared diagnostic patterns of nine psychiatrists and reported that the diagnosis of character disorders ranged from less than 50 to greater than 95 percent.

Mental Ability

The measure used most frequently in the military for estimating mental ability is the General Technical Aptitude Area (GTAA) of the Army Classification Battery (ACB). The ACB itself is composed of eleven aptitude subtests which are combined into eight areas, all of which have means of one hundred and standard deviations of twenty. The GTAA is the average of T-scores from a fifteen minute, multiple-choice vocabulary subtest and a thirty-five minute, multiple-choice arithmetic reasoning subtest. Correlations reported between Wechsler I.Q. scores and GTAA scores, or variations of them, have been about +.75, plus or minus .15 (Hedlund, 1959). Murphy and Langston (1956) reported a correlation of +.88 between Wechsler I.Q.'s and a modified GTAA score in a sample of military prisoners. In a study of 612 prisoners with below average GTAA scores, it has also been noted that very low GTAA scores tend to be an underestimate of WAIS I.Q. scores (Brodsky, 1966).

The source of the GTAA scores was the initial testing at the time the prisoners entered the military service. For most prisoners this occurred in the preceding eighteen months. To check variability between current and entering-service mental ability, eighty prisoners were readministered the GTAA subtests and a correlation of +.80 with the original testing was obtained. This suggested that entering-service GTAA scores were largely reliable. Normative data for comparison purposes were GTAA distributions for enlisted men reported by the sta-

13. GTAA Percentage Distributions of Army Prisoners and Enlisted Men, 1954–65

	Years[1]											
	1965	1964	1963	1962	1961	1960	1959	1958	1957	1956	1955	1954
Prisoners												
Below 90	33.2	32.3	38.1	37.7	37.2	42.0	41.0	49.0	50.6	62.9	58.9	63.5
90–100	46.5	47.5	45.3	42.7	43.8	39.3	39.1	36.4	35.0	20.0	30.0	27.4
110–129	17.9	18.5	14.8	16.5	16.5	16.6	18.0	13.2	12.4	16.1	10.0	8.0
130—	2.4	1.7	1.8	3.1	2.5	2.1	1.9	1.4	2.0	1.0	1.1	1.1
Enlisted Men												
Below 90	—	14.8	15.9	16.4	16.9	16.0	18.0	17.0	30.0	27.0	28.0	32.0
90–100	—	41.8	41.0	40.0	41.1	[2]	41.0	[2]	35.0	35.0	35.0	32.0
110–129	—	35.2	34.5	34.4	34.0	[2]	33.0	[2]	29.0	33.0	30.0	31.0
130—	—	8.1	8.6	9.1	8.0	[2]	8.0	[2]	6.0	5.0	7.0	5.0

[1] Enlisted men percentages from 1954 to 1960 are estimates from bar graphs in official reports.
[2] Data are incomplete for these years.

tistical section of the Office of the Provost Marshal General, Department of the Army. The scores themselves were tabulated for 1954 through 1965 and were divided into four major categories: below 90, 90–109, 110–29, and 130 and above.

The results for all USDB prisoners are shown in Table 13. A trend may be noted in the below 90, or below average, category for both prisoners and enlisted men. The incidence of this GTAA category decreased in 1965 to approximately half the 1954 level, from about two-thirds to one-third of the prisoners and from about one-third to one-seventh of the enlisted subjects. An increase appeared in the other three ability categories for both groups of subjects. Scores in the average range increased from 27.4 to 46.5 percent for prisoners and from 32.2 to 41.8 percent for the controls. Increases of more than twice the original percentages were recorded for enlisted men prisoners in the higher ability groupings, rising from 8.0 to 17.9 percent and from 1.1 to 2.4 percent in the high and very high categories respectively. Smaller increments were observed for the enlisted men in both categories, although they still maintained a large quantitative superiority overall.

There would appear to be two conclusions from these results. First, the prisoners were not drawn from a random sample of military enlisted people in terms of mental ability. That is, they varied consistently and tended to score lower on this single measure of mental ability. Second, the differences between the two groups were decreasing, in terms of absolute percentage differences within categories, with a trend present in both groups of rising ability scores. This pattern of less frequent reports of offender intelligence deficits has also been found in many recent studies of delinquent populations (Caplan, 1965).

Summary

Relatively few psychoses and neuroses were observed in one military prison setting over a twenty-five-year time period. Approximately three-fourths of thirty thousand prisoners were diagnosed as having character and behavior disorders and one-fifth were seen as having no psychiatric disease. The level of mental ability of military prisoners over a twelve-year time span was found to have increased, but remained substantially below that of their active duty counterparts.

12

Prisoner Evaluations of Correctional Programs

STANLEY L. BRODSKY

Education and vocational training have frequently been seen as the most useful correctional programs in the opinions of prisoners who have been queried while in confinement. Andry (1963) interviewed 114 short-time prisoners from the London area. He reported that they experienced little work satisfaction, but that they described their evening classes as interesting and beneficial. Glaser (1964) reported that both the work and school experiences were valued highly by subjects in several United States federal penitentiaries. "Learning a trade or getting more school credits, to help get a better job on the outside," was identified as most wanted by 82 to 94 percent of Glaser's youth subjects, depending upon when they were interviewed. This item was chosen by 38 to 59 percent of the adult prisoners studied.

The purposes of the present study were to learn how military prisoners valued a number of specific correctional programs, to compare these with staff valuations, and to investigate if length of confinement affected perception of these programs.

Method

A questionnaire was designed (Mooney and Jones, 1963) "to evaluate the Correctional Treatment Program of the United States Disciplinary Barracks by receiving comments from those who have been a part of it." It listed eighteen major institutional programs, including various educational, vocational, recreational, and therapeutic activities.

The questionnaire was administered routinely to over three thousand prisoners as they were released from early 1963 to the summer of 1966. Four selected samples were used for this study. For comparisons over time, the subjects were the last 140 prisoners who departed as of May 1963, the last two hundred as of December 1964, and the last 206 as of April 1966. Differences between subjects confined for varying lengths of time were evaluated on the last 332 prisoners released as of July 1965.

The subjects were instructed "Rank numerically which (of the following programs) were the most important or helpful to you. Number 1 would be most helpful, number 2 next, and number 18 least helpful. If you did not participate, indicate N/A." Thus ratings were obtained for given programs from the participating individuals, usually within a short period of time following the actual participation.

Results and Discussion

The ratings by prisoners as of December 1964, are presented in the left columns of Table 14. The column headed "participants" shows the number of prisoners who rated each program. For example, 98 of 200 participated in and rated the High School GED (General Educational Development) program. The "Rank" was obtained by ordering the mean scores from lowest to highest.

Several general trends were noted in the three time samples. Work assignments, counseling by an Enlisted Counselor, Prerelease, Religious activities, and Reception elicited the most participation. The fewest ratings were made for the Dale Carnegie Institute, the Associate of Arts degree program, and Alcoholics Anonymous. In addition relatively few subjects participated in the group discussions conducted by the Ft. Leavenworth officers, a program that was discontinued during the course of the study.

The High School GED program consistently averaged the highest rating over the three-year period, with about half of the subjects participating. Religious activities and Vocational Training were rated among the most favorable five activities in all three samples. Correspondence courses, Enlisted Counseling, and the College GED program were in the middle range, and consistently ranked from eighth to twelfth.

Wide fluctuations in scores and rank appeared in the Spe-

14. Prisoner and Staff Ratings of Institutional Programs

Programs	Prisoners (N = 200)		MH Staff (N = 11) Rank	Counselors (N = 13) Rank	Voc. Training Staff (N = 12) Rank
	Rank	Participants			
High School GED	1	98	2	2	2
Work Assignment	2	193	7	4	3
Religious	3	141	9	3	4
Vocational Training	4	101	1	5	1
Group Therapy—Conducted by Mental Hygiene	5	11	4	8	11
Alcoholics Anonymous	6	33	14	9	18
Dale Carnegie Institute	7	12	10	14	14
Recreation	8	108	8	11	12
USAFI Correspondence Courses	9	61	13	12	7
College GED	10	32	12	10	5
Individual Therapy— Conducted by Mental Hygiene	11	46	3	6	6
Counseling by Enlisted Counselor	12	169	5	1	10
Other Courses	13	37	18	16	17
Associate of Arts Degree, Highland Jr. College	14	10	11	15	13
Prerelease Program	15	152	16	18	15
Group Discussion— Conducted by Officers from Post	16	11	17	17	16
Special Military Training Program	17	35	15	13	9
Reception	18	174	6	7	8

cial Military Training Program, Group Therapy, the Associate of Arts program, and the Dale Carnegie Institute. The variability in the latter two activities might well be attributed to the small samples involved; however, the ranges from third to seventeenth of Special Training and from fifth to eighteenth of Group Therapy probably reflects true changes in prisoner attitudes toward these programs.

At the middle point of the three-year period similar program ratings were obtained from staff groups. Mental Hygiene, Enlisted Counselors, and Vocational Training staff members were asked to rank in order from one to eighteen those programs they personally felt were most helpful to the prisoners. Table 14 presents the comparison between staff and prisoner ratings.

There was agreement among staff and prisoners in rating High School GED and Vocational Training high, and Other Courses, Associate of Arts degree program, Prerelease, and Group Discussion low. Compared to prisoner ratings, the staff viewed Individual Therapy, Enlisted Counseling, and Special Military Training as more helpful, and Alcoholics Anonymous and the Dale Carnegie Institute as less helpful. The higher staff ratings for therapy and counseling may be a sign of the importance and prestige attached by staff to the psychological treatment approach of dealing with offenders.

Length of confinement was investigated by dividing the last 332 prisoners who had left as of July 1965, into four groups: Longs, or those who had been confined over one year; Mediums, 6 months to a year; Shorts, four to six months; and Short-Shorts, under four months. There were 50, 134, 95, and 53 subjects, respectively, in these groups.

Table 15 shows the program ratings and participation. The Dale Carnegie Institute was ranked highly overall. This finding was divergent from other ratings of this activity and may reflect the proximity in time of the Institute and the ratings sampled. Religious Activities, Work Assignments, and Alcoholics Anonymous were others uniformly rated high.

Some major differences were present between the groups. Individual Therapy was rated positively only by the Longs, while Group Therapy was rated much higher by the Longs and

15. *Institutional Program Ratings by Prisoners Following Differing Lengths of Confinement*

	Confinement							
	Longs (over 1 yr.) N = 50		Mediums (6 mos.–1 yr.) N = 134		Shorts (4–6 mos.) N = 95		Short-Shorts (less than 4 mos.) N = 53	
Programs	Rank	Participants	Rank	Participants	Rank	Participants	Rank	Participants
Dale Carnegie Institute	1	9	3	7	6	5	1	3
Religious	2	33	4	93	1	60	2	35
Work Assignment	3	47	2	130	2	91	5	47
Alcoholics Anonymous	4	12	6	28	8	17	3	5
Individual Therapy— Conducted by Mental Hygiene	5	14	17	29	17	28	14	17
Associate of Arts Degree, Highland Jr. College	6	10	5	10	15	5	18	1
Group Therapy— Conducted by Mental Hygiene	7	12	8	26	16	17	13	7
High School GED	8	28	1	7	7	36	6	23
Other Courses	9	17	10	25	12	16	17	3
Vocational Training	10	26	7	64	3	49	11	12
Recreation	11	31	12	83	5	51	8	31
College GED	12	17	9	22	9	12	9	3
Counseling by Enlisted Counselor	13	45	14	115	11	85	12	38
Special Military Training	14	8	13	28	13	16	7	8
Reception	15	47	15	118	10	86	10	41
Prerelease Program	16	39	16	110	14	64	16	25
USAFI Correspondence	17	29	11	40	4	17	4	12
Group Discussion— Conducted by Officers from Post	18	5	18	11	18	8	15	5

Mediums than by the shorter-term groups. These findings indicate that among these groups some minimal confinement and participation time was necessary before those receiving psychotherapy perceived this experience positively. In a similar manner the low ratings of the Associate of Arts program by the shorter-term prisoners and high ratings by the longer-term subjects may reflect differences in involvement and completion.

Positive ratings by short-termers and negative or neutral ratings by long-termers were noted for the Recreation and Correspondence Courses Activities. Both activities require no closure, and indeed their open-ended nature may account for this finding. That is, they require minimal commitment to the acquisition of prisoner roles and in both cases may represent direct continuation of pre-confinement behavior.

These results would also appear to be associated with certain other characteristics of the prisoner population. The relatively high rating of the Special Military Training Program by Short-Shorts may result from the greater probability of these individuals to be confined without a discharge, to be restored to military duty, and thus to be experiencing this training as more appropriate to future plans and goals. The very small number of shorter-term prisoners participating in programs such as the Dale Carnegie Institute, Alcoholics Anonymous, and College GED make such ratings less reliable and meaningful. Furthermore some items may have been misinterpreted. The fact that some prisoners who rated Group Discussion had arrived after this program was discontinued suggests that they interpreted it to refer to casual, unprogrammed group discussions with post officers. Similarly all prisoners are seen diagnostically at least three times by Mental Hygiene staff and they may have perceived such experiences as therapy. Caution must be used in interpreting the differing results as caused by length of confinement. Third factors, such as preselected, offense-related personality variables may underlie such apparent findings.

Summary and Conclusions

A release questionnaire was used over a three-year period with departing prisoners, and relative program evaluations were made at different points in time, between staff and prisoner groups, and between prisoners confined for varying sentences. The data were interpreted on the basis of program ranking, and it was observed that religious, vocational, and educational activities were felt to be most helpful. The results were in substantial agreement with other studies in this respect.

Some notable discrepancies were present between various staff and prisoner subgroup ratings; these differences could provide a beginning for reevaluating staff views of institutional programs. In a like fashion the differential perceptions by prisoners confined for varying times can lead to activity reevaluations, with special emphasis on the needs of these specific prisoner subgroups.

13

After They Leave: A Vocational Follow-up Study of Former Prisoners

JOHN D. NICHOLS *and*
STANLEY L. BRODSKY

In a military prison there are two built-in, but somewhat limited, follow-up systems: parole and restoration to duty. Very few parolees are returned for parole violation and little research has been performed with the successful parolees. Even fewer of those who are restored to active duty return to confinement as a result of further courts-martial; those who are restored successfully are generally rated as excellent soldiers and usually receive honorable discharges.

No such automatic system exists in the case of vocational training follow-ups. The purpose of the present paper is to briefly describe one military prison's approach to vocational training and recognition and to report on the vocational aftermaths of this training.

Vocational Training and Certification

Approximately one-fourth of the prisoners at the United States Disciplinary Barracks, Ft. Leavenworth, Kansas are assigned to work officially designated as vocational training. This includes training in Auto Mechanics, Barbering, Printing, Screen-Process Printing, Sheet Metal, Machine, Shoe Repair, Upholstery, and Radio-TV Repair Shops. Other trades are added and deleted from time to time according to changing institutional interests and prisoner population. The actual selection and assignment of individual prisoners to specific shops is usually dependent upon the prisoner's previous experience in the trade, his interest in learning and working in the trade now and in the future, and the need for personnel in the shops. The training itself is organized for individuals unfamiliar with the trade; regular class periods on the job and related trade classes in the evening are part of the program.

In addition to those prisoners in the vocational training details, almost 40 percent of the prisoners work in positions that are necessary to institutional maintenance and operations. These include, but are not limited to, the Mess Hall, Laundry, Carpenter Shop, Electric Shop, Plumbing Shop, and Clothing Factory. Training in these shops is not as formal as in the vocational details, but nevertheless necessity dictates that the various skills must be taught in a planned, step-by-step procedure.

For many years a certificate has been given to trained prisoners, which certified the type and amount of training received while in confinement. At one time the certificate was printed with the heading in large letters—"UNITED STATES DISCIPLINARY BARRACKS." It was not popularly received and released prisoners asked for records that did not emphasize the USDB as the place of training.

In 1954, officials from the Kansas State Board of Vocational Education visited the USDB and inspected the vocational training facilities. Detailed information was provided for them regarding the operation of the Disciplinary Barracks in general, and the vocational training program in particular.

A mutually acceptable *Certificate of Accomplishment* was developed with the Kansas Board that documented the number of hours of training, the specific areas of training, and the quality of the trainee's work. Although at first certificates were limited to training in the vocational details, they were soon extended to cover training for all of the details in the institution. The training was recorded in the files of the Kansas board, the certificates signed, and then returned to the trained prisoners. Thus this certificate constituted recognition by an established training agency not identified with the prison. In the present study it was specifically those prisoners who had received Certificates of Accomplishment who were the subjects of interest and the goal was to evaluate the post-release utilization of this certified training.

Method

Eight hundred and twelve (812) questionnaires were mailed to released prisoners who had received a *Certificate of Accomplishment* during the three and one-half-year period from July 1960 to December 1963. The questionnaires were sent to prisoners at periods from two to twelve months following their release. Of the 812 questionnaires sent out, 117 were returned unclaimed. A total of 214 questionnaires were returned answered, or 30.8 percent of the 695 assumed received. The project was continued with the awareness that the subjects answering represented a highly selective sampling that did not necessarily reflect on all the subjects receiving certificates.

The following questions were sent with a letter of explanation. Space was provided for the answers and a franked, self-addressed return envelope enclosed.

 1. Have you ever secured employment in your training field?
 2. If so, are you now employed in this field?
 3. If not employed in this field, will you attempt to find such employment?
 4. Have you ever used this training in homecraft or as a hobby?
 5. How do you rate this training? Having considerable value? Some value? Little or no value?
 6. If you have been employed in your field of training, how do you think your employer rated your training? Having considerable value? Some value? Little or no value?
 7. Has any trade union ever given you any credit for your training? If so, how much?
 8. Have you ever secured employment in a field related to your training field? If so, what field?
 9. If employed, what is your present job?
 10. Please give us any comments or suggestions which you think will help us evaluate or improve our training program.

The results of the returned questionnaires were summarized and the following information was tabulated for the returned questionnaires: type of institutional training, number

16. Response of Released Prisoners to Questionnaire by Number and by Type of Training Received in Prison

Training	Number Assumed Received	Number Returned	Percent Returned
Vocational Training			
Auto Mechanics	33	11	33.3
Barbering	87	27	31.0
Greenhouse	8	3	37.5
Landscape Gardening	6	3	50.0
Photography	4	1	25.0
Printing	25	5	20.0
Screen-Process Printing	52	17	32.7
Sheet Metal	58	13	22.4
Shoe Repair	39	12	30.8
Upholstering	59	17	28.8
Woodworking (Vocational)	9	3	33.3
Administration and Clerical	52	18	34.6
Subtotal	432	130	30.1
Institutional Maintenance			
Carpentry	25	6	24.0
Clothing Manufacturing	67	20	29.9
Drafting	9	4	44.4
Dry Cleaning	6	1	16.7
Electrician	25	11	44.0
Food Service	24	7	29.2
Laundry	7	3	42.9
Machine Shop	5	3	60.0
Masonry	27	10	37.0
Painting	16	4	25.0
Plumbing	16	6	37.5
Typewriter Repair	13	2	15.4
Woodworking (Maintenance)	13	3	23.1
Miscellaneous	10	4	40.0
Subtotal	263	84	31.9
Total	695	214	30.8

of ex-prisoner respondents from the different shops, present location of the ex-prisoner, and a summary of the other questionnaire items.

Results and Discussion

Table 16 illustrates the number of subjects trained by each shop who were assumed to have received questionnaires and the response percentage by shops.

The highest rates of response were from subjects who had received certificates in the Machine Shop, Landscape Gardening, Drafting, Electric Shop and Laundry. The lowest return rates were from subjects certified by the Typewriter Repair detail, Dry-Cleaning plant, Print shop, Sheet Metal shop, and the Maintenance Woodworking shop. Contrary to expectations, about the same percentages of returns were received from vocational training details as from the other institutional details.

What the ex-prisoners were actually doing after release is shown in Table 17. About 80 percent of the men responding were employed, were in the service, or were students. About 20 percent said they were unemployed, did not state whether they were employed or not, or were in confinement.

The largest single occupation of the respondents was factory work, and no equivalent certification was issued at the USDB for this work. All 19 of the subjects who were currently employed in Shoe Repair, Upholstery, Barbering, and Screen-Process Printing had received training certificates for these skills while confined. Eleven of the 13 former prisoners working in Auto Mechanics or as printers, had been certified in these areas. Overall, 54 of the 214 subjects, or 25.2 percent, were currently employed in the field in which they had been trained while confined.

When the occupations were classified by the major groups in the *Dictionary of Occupational Titles*, a distinct pattern appeared. Of the 53 subjects employed in skilled occupations, 39 had been certified in these training fields at the USDB. Five of the 18 ex-prisoners in professional and managerial positions had been certified, and none of the 16 individuals working in

17. Current Employment or Status at Time of Answering Questionnaire for 214 Respondents

Present Occupation	Number	Same Training USDB
Professional and Managerial		
Accountant	2	—
Artist	2	1
Auditor	1	—
Draftsman	3	2
Manager, Cafe	1	—
Office Manager	2	—
Photographer	1	1
Plant Manager	1	—
Quality Control Supervisor	1	—
Service Manager, Mobile Home	1	—
Superintendent Construction	1	—
Supply Manager	1	—
Teacher	1	1
Total	18	5
Clerical and Sales		
Clerical Work	2	—
Salesman	6	—
Auto Parts Sales	1	—
Shipping Clerk	5	—
Warehouseman	2	—
Total	16	—
Service Occupations		
Barber	6	6
Bartender	1	—
Cook	5	1
Private Investigator	1	—
Total	13	7
Agriculture		
Farming	6	1
Total	6	1
Skilled Occupations		
Aircraft Electrician	1	—
Auto Mechanic	6	5
Baker	3	2
Body and Fender Work	1	—

17. Current Employment or Status at Time of Answering Questionnaire for 214 Respondents—continued

Present Occupation	Number	Same Training USDB
Bricklayer	1	1
Cabinetmaker	2	2
Carpenter	3	1
Electrician	2	2
Machinist	4	1
Painter	1	1
Plasterer	1	—
Plumber	2	2
Printer	5	4
Repairman, Coin Machines	1	—
Screen-Process Printing	3	3
Sheet Metal Worker	3	2
Shoe Repairing	6	6
Steelworker	1	—
Typewriter Repair	2	2
Upholsterer	4	4
Welder	1	1
Total	53	39
Semiskilled Occupations		
Cab Driver	1	—
Clothing Manufacturing	2	2
Factory Work	24	—
Heavy Equipment Operator	1	—
Machinist Helper	1	—
Service Station Attendant	4	—
Truck Driver	2	—
Total	35	2
Unskilled Occupations		
Construction Worker	1	—
Laborer	3	—
Total	4	—
Miscellaneous		
Unemployed	21	—
In Army or Air Force	20	—
Student	4	—
In Confinement	5	—
Work Information Not Available	19	—
Total	69	—

clerical and sales occupations. The semiskilled occupations produced a low rate, with only two of 35 people employed in certified skills.

Although 54 were employed in their training field at the
time of responding, 95 of the 214 subjects, or 44 percent, indicated that they had been employed at some time in their field
of training. The individual comments of those who had been
but were not now employed in a USDB-trained skill suggested
that some had difficulty holding a position, and others had gone
on to better jobs.

A total of 87 men of the 214 indicated they would attempt
to find employment in the field in which they were trained and
in which they were now not employed. Some of these men were
in the service, a few in jail, some unemployed, and some employed in jobs they did not particularly like. Over one hundred
men indicated that they had used their training skills as a hobby
or for work around the house.

A total of 161 reported that they felt the training had "considerable" value. Ten reported "little or no value." This supports the hypothesis that the ones who answered the questionnaire had positive feelings toward the USDB training experience. Eighteen subjects stated that they were given credit by a
union; however this finding is difficult to interpret since there
was no information utilized regarding the degree of unionization
of the varying jobs studied.

The reporting of statistical data alone omits the very valu-
able individual comments and experiences of the former prisoners. Therefore, samples of returned questionnaires are presented here to communicate some of the feelings that actually
accompanied these reports. Approximately three out of every
four of the returned forms contained comments or suggestions.
Many questionnaires contained favorable comments such as the
following:

> "I think the training program you have is very good the way it is."
> "I think the barber training I have received is the best anyone
> could ask for. As far as suggestions I have none because you have
> the best equipment and instructor you could find anywhere. I want
> to thank you and Mr. Carnoli both for the help you have given
> me."

Some letters from individuals returned to the service told of plans to use their training in the future:

> "I feel that the training I received in confinement prepared me for my life on the outside if I had returned as a civilian. Since I am still in the Army I feel that if I do not make the service a career this training will come in handy."

Several subjects did make suggestions, such as the following:

> "excellent training program. One minor suggestion—emphasis should be placed on speed as well as quality. This factor carries great weight." "The men should be given a chance to lay more blocks and brick, also they should be taught how to set tile."

Some men mentioned profiting from some other aspect of their prison experience such as securing an Associate of Arts Degree. Others exhibited in their replies that they could have profited from more academic schooling:

> "I just can give you a short comment cause my Inglish isn't too well. I think that the training that I took is with a good benefit to me cause I work for the period of four (4) months in a shoe factory. My suggestion is that the man in charge of the training of the shoe repairman, he supost to give more training to the new man, so he can learn the work perfet. In some case lot of man go to the vocational training of shoe maker to pass the time. That all I can said."

One impression was that help should be given some men being released in getting and holding a job. Experience with giving a prerelease talk on this subject has given the authors the impression hat men about to be released care little about discussing such topics. However, to quote one more respondent.

> "I would like to find a job in Auto Mechanics. If you should hear of a job in this area I sure appreciate it if you would let me know."

Implications and Limitations

A] It is felt that studying whether the training of prisoners resulted in employment when released has opened up avenues for establishing other appropriate training facilities for prisoners. The high factory- and office-work frequencies point to possible new training programs in these areas as well as possibly suggesting deficits in the original areas of training for these men.

B] About 40 of the 214 men responding were either unemployed (21) and said so, or did not state what they were doing and most likely were not employed (19). This seems to point up the need not only for teaching skills, but also simultaneously working with prisoner attitudes and perseverance.

C] The highest success rate occurred in the skilled occupations in terms of utilization of training. This suggested that emphasis in training in skilled trades is of distinct value.

D] There is a methodological question in this study with reference to how much of the certified skill is institutionally acquired. That is, some individuals are skilled prior to confinement and the receipt of a certificate may only identify existing skills for such people. The personal observations of the authors is that relatively few prisoners fall within this category.

E] It must be observed that these results can only be generalized to a limited degree. The modest return rate limits its application to other settings.

Summary

The purpose of this study was to see if former military prisoners used training received while confined. Two hundred and fourteen ex-prisoners, or 30.8 percent of the group located, returned questionnaires concerning their current jobs, use of institution-acquired vocational skills and attitudes toward their training. The ex-prisoners working in Barbering, Shoe Repair, Upholstery, and Screen-Process Printing all had been certified as skilled in those areas while confined. Nearly half of the subjects had, at some time, secured employment in the field in which they had been trained, and approximately 75 percent felt that their training had been "of considerable value." The implications of these findings were discussed with reference to present and future programs.

14

Employer Attitudes Toward Hiring Dishonorably Discharged Servicemen

LEONARD J. HIPPCHEN

In attempting to assist Air Force retrainees in their re-socialization, two kinds of situations present continuing problems. One relates to retrainees who are not highly motivated to return to duty, and the other relates to retrainees who are to be discharged to civilian life.

Retrainees who are in a state of uncertainty regarding their desire to return to military or civilian life are blocked from further progress. In these situations, the staff usually attempts to help the retrainee consider all of the pros and cons of each direction which he might take. For therapeutic reasons, it is important that the retrainee make his own decision. Staff members have been hampered by not having recent, accurate information on employment problems of dischargees, which could be added to the factors being reviewed by the retrainee in such a way as to encourage him to give full, realistic consideration to return to duty.

In the situation where the decision has been made both by the staff and the retrainee that he and the Air Force would best be served by his return to civilian life, information on factors affecting his employment adjustment are also needed. Counseling in this situation is directed toward assisting the retrainee to develop a plan to cope with the various problems which he will be facing. Employment typically is a problem of great concern. Realistic planning at this point requires accurate information on the factors involved with the dischargee's successful employment in the civilian community.

A review of the literature indicates that studies of the employment problems of offenders returning to civilian life have been limited to those involving release from civilian prisons (Hannum, 1960; McSally, 1960; Melichercik, 1956; Wise, 1960). Although the findings of these studies are helpful, they have limited value, since the two situations of military and civilian offenses are not entirely comparable and are likely to be perceived differently by possible employers. The offenses typically vary in severity, and also there are many types of military offenses which would not be a civilian offense, such as Absent Without Leave, Abuse of Authority, Failure to Obey an Order, etc.

PURPOSE OF THE STUDY

The purpose of this study is to gather information on the factors affecting the civilian employment of servicemen discharged under other than honorable conditions.

Specifically, the study attempts to answer the following questions:

1] What are the chances of servicemen discharged under other than honorable conditions being considered for employment, and for what kinds of jobs and with what size firms are they *most* likely to be considered for employment?

2] For what reasons are they likely not to be considered for employment?

3] If they are considered for employment, what factors will employers be *most* favorably impressed with, and what factors will they be *least* favorably impressed with?

4] If they are considered for employment, for what kinds of jobs and with what size firms are they *most* likely to qualify? For what kinds of jobs and with what size firms are they *least* likely to qualify?

5] What is the extent of the problem of employment for servicemen discharged under other than honorable conditions, and what suggestions would employers make to increase the employment probabilities of such persons?

Findings

The survey returns were divided into nine business classifications and into large and medium-small size firms. The business classifications include: *1*] Retail Trade; *2*] Services; *3*] Government; *4*] Transportation, Public Utilities; *5*] Manufacturing; *6*] Construction; *7*] Wholesale Trade; *8*] Finance, Insurance, and Real Estate; and *9*] Petroleum, Gas Production, and Mining. Large firms are defined as those employing twenty-five-plus employees in the Retail Trade, Services, and Finance, Insurance, Real Estate classifications, and those employing one hundred-plus employees in the Manufacturing Classification. Under twenty-five employees and under one hundred employees define the firms in the medium-small groups for these classifications. Breakdowns were not made for the other five business classifications because of the relatively small number of respondents in these categories.

PROPORTION OF FIRMS HAVING
POLICIES FORBIDDING AND ALLOWING
CONSIDERATION FOR HIRING

Question 1 asked: "Do the policies of your company allow you to consider for employment a person who has been discharged under other than honorable conditions from any of the Armed Services?"

The responses to this question indicate that 53 percent of the firms in the population studied have policies which do not allow consideration for employment of servicemen discharged under other than honorable conditions; 47 percent will consider such persons.

Firms in the business classifications of Government, Petroleum, Gas Production, Mining, Transportation, and Public Utilities appear to be *most* willing to *consider* such persons.

However, the survey reveals that such persons will experience difficulty in being hired even by these firms, primarily because these firms tend to have the most rigid screening criteria for applicants. Firms in Finance, Insurance, Real Estate, and Services classifications appear *least* willing to *consider* such persons, primarily because of lack of trust.

In differentiating between large and medium-small size firms, large Retail Trade and medium-small Manufacturing firms appear to be more willing than the average to consider the range of employment applicants dealt with in this study. This expressed attitude appears to be related to their greater need for relatively unskilled personnel; that is, they would consider such persons primarily for positions requiring only limited skills.

REASONS POLICIES FORBID
CONSIDERATION FOR HIRING

Question 2 asked: "Please list the major reason(s) why your company policies do not allow you to consider these persons for employment, in order of importance."

The reason most frequently given in answer to this question is that firms do not want to risk hiring a person of questionable moral character, especially when other qualified persons are readily available. This attitude is particularly evident among those firms requiring bonding or licensing of employees.

Other firms state that they would not consider such persons for hire because the nature of their business requires persons who are responsible, who are emotionally stable, and who can work well with other employees and with the people whom they serve.

Several firms stated that they have had unsatisfactory past experience in hiring such persons, and that they now would not hire anyone without having verified information on their background. Their complaint is that they are not able to secure adequate background information on this type of applicant, and they have decided not to consider any of them for hire.

Finally, several firms expressed this attitude: "If he can't serve his country, he can't work for me!"

RANKING OF FACTORS FAVORABLE AND UNFAVORABLE FOR HIRING, BY BUSINESS CLASSIFICATION

Questions 3 and *4* asked those who would consider service-men discharged under other than honorable conditions to list, in order of importance, the three most important favorable and unfavorable factors in their consideration to hire or not to hire such persons. Analysis of the responses showed that the answers could be grouped under the following eleven headings: Good or Poor Moral Character; Good or Poor Background; Successful or Unsuccessful Work Experience; Personable or Unpersonable; Socially Adept or Inept; Responsible or Irresponsible; Desire or Lack of Desire to Get Ahead; Desire or Lack of Desire for Self-Improvement; Adequate or Inadequate Training or Education, Good or Poor Adjustment Capacity; and Good and Poor Aptitude for the Job.

The *favorable* factor responses are summarized in Table 18. which shows the three highest-ranked favorable factors for each of the nine business classifications.

Five of the nine business groups listed Good Moral Character as the most *favorable* factor. The business classification firms of Government, Finance, Insurance, Real Estate showed greatest concern with this factor. Proving good moral character appears to be the greatest obstacle to be overcome by these ex-servicemen. Firms appear, however, to be willing to give such persons consideration if they can show mitigating circumstances surrounding their offense of discharge, especially, young, first-offenders, who realize their mistake and are anxious to prove themselves, even if it means taking a routine or non-skilled job for a trial period. However, they are not apt to be given a position of trust or high responsibility initially.

Construction and Wholesale Trade firms rank the most *favorable* factor as Successful Work Experience. Particularly for unskilled jobs, these firms appear to be willing to give such persons a trial if they can show that they have been effective in the performance of similar work for other firms. An Air Force offender, thus, would stand a better chance for employment in these areas, particularly if he had performed effectively in this type of work in the Air Force or previous to his entry into the Service.

18. *Three Highest Ranked Factors Favorable for Hiring, by Business Classification*

Business	First	Second	Third
Construction	Successful Work Experience	Desire to Get Ahead	Good Moral Character
Finance, Insurance, Real Estate	Good Moral Character	Socially Adept	Responsible
Government	Good Moral Character	Good Adjustment Capacity	Successful Work Experience
Manufacturing	Good Moral Character	Adequate Training Education	Socially Adept
Petroleum, Gas, Mining	Socially Adept	Good Moral Character	Adequate Training Education
Retail Trade	Good Moral Character	Desire to Get Ahead	Successful Work Experience
Services	Good Moral Character	Successful Work Experience	Socially Adept
Transportation, Public Utilities	Socially Adept	Good Moral Character	Desire to Get Ahead
Wholesale Trade	Successful Work Experience	Socially Adept	Adequate Training Experience

The classification groups of Transportation, Public Utilities, Petroleum, Gas Production, and Mining rank highest the *favorable* factor of Social Adeptness. These and other firms ranking this factor high are most concerned with their public reputation, with the employee's ability to make a good impression on the persons whom they serve, and with the firm. Persons with records of antisocial behavior, it would appear, would not be considered seriously for employment by these types of firms, unless on a trial basis for positions of lesser responsibility and social demands.

The *unfavorable* factor responses are summarized in Table

19. Again, firms show greatest concern with the factors of moral character, social behavior, and work experience, although the order of the second and third ranked factors are reversed.

19. *Three Highest Ranked Factors Unfavorable for Hiring, by Business Classification*

Business	First	Second	Third
Construction	Unsuccessful Work Experience	Socially Inept	Lack of Desire to Get Ahead
Finance, Insurance, Real Estate	Socially Inept	Poor Moral Character	Irresponsible
Government	Poor Moral Character	Poor Adjustment Capacity	Lack of Desire for Self-Improvement
Manufacturing	Poor Moral Character	Socially Inept	Poor Adjustment Capacity
Petroleum, Gas, Mining	Socially Inept	Poor Moral Character	Inadequate Training Education
Retail Trade	Poor Moral Character	Socially Inept	Poor Adjustment Capacity
Services	Poor Moral Character	Socially Inept	Irresponsible
Transportation, Public Utilities	Socially Inept	Poor Moral Character	Poor Adjustment Capacity
Wholesale Trade	Unsuccessful Work Experience	Socially Inept	Poor Moral Character

The findings suggest that offenders would experience the greatest difficulty in being employed because of questions relating to their moral character and social behavior. Even in overcoming these obstacles and in being hired by firms concerned with these factors, they probably would be on a rigid trial basis. They probably would have better opportunity for employment, at least initially, among firms concerned primarily with skills which they might possess or with demonstrated work experience.

RANKING OF FACTORS FAVORABLE AND
UNFAVORABLE FOR HIRING, BY
SIZE OF BUSINESS FIRM

The response data to questions #3 and #4 also were
analyzed for four business classification groups by size of firm.
The three highest-ranked factors which were favorable and
unfavorable for hiring were summarized by two firm size groupings: large and medium-small.

Both large and medium-small size firms are concerned with
the Moral Character and Social Adeptness of applicants. However, large firms tend also to consider important *favorable* factors to include Responsibility and Aptitude for the Job, whereas
medium-small firms *favor* Successful Work Experience and
Desire for Self-Improvement. Further, large firms tend also to
consider important *unfavorable* factors to include Poor Personality, Irresponsibility, and Lack of Desire to Get Ahead; whereas
medium-small firms view *unfavorable* factors to include Unsuccessful Work Experience and Lack of Training or Education.

In addition to these total differentiating factors between
large and medium-small size firms, the study uncovered numerous differences between the large and medium-small firms of
the four business classification groups which were analyzed.

Large firms in the Retail Trade class appear to be most
concerned with such factors as Desire to Get Ahead, Personality,
Social Adeptness and Job Aptitude, whereas the medium-small
firms appear to be most interested in Work Experience, Moral
Character, Training Skills or Education, and Desire for Self-
Improvement.

Large firms in the Service classification appear to be most
concerned with the factors of Social Ability, Responsibility and
Education; whereas the medium-small firms tend to be more
interested in Moral Character, Background, Work Experience
and the Desire to Get Ahead.

Large firms in the Manufacturing classification appear
to be most concerned with such factors as Moral Character,

Background, Work Experience, and Responsibility; whereas medium-small firms tend to look for the factors of Social Adeptness, Desire to Get Ahead, and Training or Education.

Large firms in the Finance, Insurance, Real Estate classification tend to be most concerned with such factors as Moral Character and Responsibility; whereas medium-small firms tend to be concerned with Personality, Social Ability, Desire to Get Ahead, and Training or Education.

These data suggest, in general, that offenders would have equal difficulty being hired by both large and medium-small firms in regard to the criteria of moral character and social adeptness. However, those who can demonstrate responsibility and have good aptitude for the job are most apt to be hired by large firms; and those who show desire for self-improvement and who have had successful work experience are more apt to be hired by medium-small size firms.

Recommendations

Question #5 in the survey asked the respondents to make general comments on the problem or suggestions for improving the employment potentials of persons discharged from the Armed Forces under other than honorable conditions.

1] The suggestion most frequently made is that the Armed Forces should provide the business community, on a case request basis, with specific information on the nature of the offense or circumstances surrounding the cause of the receipt of a discharge under other than honorable conditions. Numerous firms stated that this information would greatly aid their earnest attempts to give *deserving* ex-servicemen a chance to prove themselves.

2] A number of firms suggest that the Armed Forces should provide adequate personal and employment counseling to each dischargee before release to the civilian community. These firms claim that many of these ex-servicemen have no *idea* of the problems with which they will need to cope, and that this inability increases the probability of their becoming involved in criminal acts.

3] Some firms express the view that a great aid would be the publication, by the Armed Forces, of a pamphlet which would provide information on the various types, together with degrees of severity, of military offenses and discharges. There appears to be a general lack of knowledge of the types of offenses that servicemen typically tend to become involved in and the reasons behind this involvement. There also appears to be a general lack of knowledge of the various kinds of offenses or other factors associated with various discharge types. This information is needed by the business community in order to be able to understand the probable relationship between the other than honorable discharge types and employment success with their firms.

4] Two firms suggest that the military should not release servicemen to the civilian community with other than honorable discharges. The inference here is that servicemen should be aided in their problems and retained until they perform satisfactorily for the entire period of their enlistments.

Conclusions

The range and types of suggestions offered by the business community in this survey indicate that there exists considerable *concern* and interest in the employment problems faced by servicemen discharged under other than honorable conditions. However, the survey also suggests that offenders, in many instances, are experiencing undue difficulties in qualifying for any except fringe-type jobs, because of inadequate understanding and lack of information in the business community.

The findings of this study indicate that the 3320th Retraining Group should increase its efforts to assist dischargees to qualify for employment in returning to the civilian community. These efforts can be directed toward increased cooperation with employment and hiring agencies in the local community and an increased emphasis on the counseling of dischargees. Also, the obstacles to be faced by servicemen discharged under other than honorable conditions should be brought forcefully to the attention of all retrainees early in the program so that they can be aided in their motivation to return to duty and successfully complete their enlistment term.

BIBLIOGRAPHY
INDEX

BIBLIOGRAPHY OF
MILITARY CORRECTIONS

Abrahams, J. & McCorkle, L. W. Group psychotherapy at an Army rehabilitation center. *Diseases of the Nervous System,* 1947, *8,* 50–62.

Abrahams, J. & McCorkle, L. W. Analysis of a prison disturbance. *Journal of Abnormal and Social Psychology,* 1947, *42,* 330–41.

Aita, J. A. Efficiency of brief clinical interview method in predicting adjustments; a 5-year-follow-up study of 304 Army inductees. *Archives of Neurology and Psychiatry,* 1949, *61,* 170–76.

Andry, R. G. *The Short-Term Prisoner.* London: Stevens and Sons, 1963.

Ash, P. The Reliability of psychiatric diagnoses. *Journal of Abnormal and Social Psychology,* 1949, *44,* 272–76.

Ballard, K. B., Bobinski, C. A., & Grant, J. D. A pilot study of factors in retraining which change delinquency attitudes. Third technical report. San Diego; United States Naval Retraining Command, Camp Elliott, January 1956.

Baynes, J. *Morale. A Study of Men and Courage.* London: Cassell, 1967.

Bennett, J. V. Criminal record as a bar to military service. *Federal Probation,* 1941, *5,* (3), 6–8.

Berman, H. J. *Justice in Russia.* Cambridge: Harvard University Press, 1950.

Blackman, S., Speshock, M. J., & Boyd, R. C. Environmental influences on parolee success. *Military Medicine,* 1963, *128,* 772–75.

Blaisdell, O. D. The therapeutic value of religion in rehabilitation. *Military Police Journal,* 1963, *12* (9), 16–18.

Bluestone, H. & Perkins, M. E. Community Psychiatry in a correctional system. *American Journal of Corrections,* 1965, 27 (2), 10–13.

Boshes, D. & Hermann, J. The Naval delinquent. *Journal of Criminal Law and Criminology,* 1947, *38,* 218–34.

Brickenstein, R. Zur strafrechtlichen Zurechnungsfahigkeit und weiteren Dienstfahigkeit straffallig gewordener Soldaten. *Nervenarzt,* 1965, *36* (1), 32–39.

Brief history of the U.S. Naval Disciplinary Command. In *Welcome Aboard,* U.S. Naval Disciplinary Command pamphlet, undated.

Briggs, D. L. Behavioral inadequacies among Naval recruits. *Military Medicine,* 1958, *123,* 449–53.

Broder, G. J. Multidisciplinary approach to prisoner rehabilitation in the

Air Force. Presented at the annual meeting of the Association of Military Surgeons, Washington, D.C., November, 1965.

Brodsky, I. Disciplinary Barracks. In H. S. Maas (Ed.), *Adventures in Mental Health.* New York: Columbia University Press, 1951. Pp. 99–117.

Brodsky, I. AWOL and after. *Survey Mid-Monthly,* 1956, *80,* 138–41.

Brodsky, S. L. Reliability and interpretation of the GT score in assessing the military prisoner. Project *3–65,* The Council for Research and Evaluation, United States Disciplinary Barracks, 1965.

Brodsky, S. L., & Grossheim, P. W. Custodial personnel at the USDB. *Military Police Journal,* 1965, *15* (4), 10–11.

Brodsky, S. L. Mehaffey, T. H. and Rhoads, R. H. Biographical and psychodiagnostic dimensions of behavioral adjustment to the military prison. *Military Medicine,* 1965, *130,* 480–84.

Brodsky, S. L. The Army Classification Battery GT score as a measure of intelligence in a military prisoner population. *Journal of Clinical Psychology,* 1966, 22, 81–84.

Brodsky, S. L. Some observations of a clinical psychologist in a military penal setting. *Corrective Psychiatry and Journal of Social Therapy,* 1966, *12,* 446–71.

Brodsky, S. L. & Komaridis, G. W. Military prisonization. *Military Police Journal,* 1966, *15* (12), 8–9.

Brodsky, S. L. *Collected Papers in Prison Psychology,* Publication *6–66,* Council for Research and Evaluation, U.S. Disciplinary Barracks, 1967.

Brodsky, S. L. & Brodsky, Annette M. Hand test indicators of antisocial behavior. *Journal of Projective Techniques and Personality Assessment,* 1967, *31* (5), 36–39.

Brodsky, S. L. & Couch, S. A. An approach to correctional consultation. *Military Police Journal,* 1967, *17* (1), 12–13.

Brodsky, S. L. & Eggleston, N. E. Role Perceptions in the Military Prison Publication *2–65,* Council for Research and Evaluation, 1967.

Brodsky, S. L. Excessive dispensary users in the military prison. *Military Medicine,* 1968, *133,* 368–71 (reprinted in *Correctional Psychologist,* 1968, *3* (5), 20–21).

Brodsky, S. L. & Komaridis, G. V. Self-disclosure in prisoners. *Psychological Reports,* 1968, *23,* 403–7.

Bromberg, W., Apuzzo, A. A., & Locke, B. Psychologic study of desertion and overleave in Navy. *United States Navy Medical Bulletin,* 1945, *44,* 558–68.

Burkett, J. W. Predicting the efficiency of problem soldiers. *United States Armed Forces Medical Journal,* 1953, *4,* 67–69.

Bushard, B. L. & Dahlgren, A. W. A technic for military delinquency management. *United States Armed Forces Medical Journal,* 1957, *8,* 1616–31 and 1745–60 (two parts).

Cain, L. F. & Richmond, M. S. The success and failure of 926 Naval offenders. *Journal of Criminal Law and Criminology*, 1947, *37*, 390–407.

Campbell, D. T. & McCormack, T. H. Military experience and attitudes toward authority. *American Journal of Sociology*, 1957, *62*, 482–90.

Canter, F. M. & Canter, A. N. Authoritarian attitudes and adjustment in a military situation. *United States Armed Forces Medical Journal*, 1957, *8*, 1201–7.

Caplan, N. S. Intellectual functioning. In H. C. Quay (Ed.), *Juvenile Delinquency: Research and Theory*. Princeton, N.J.: Van Nostrand, 1965, 100–138.

Carmichael, L. & Meade, L. C. (Eds.). *The Selection of Military Manpower*. National Academy of Sciences, National Research Council, Washington, D.C., 1957.

Carr, L. J. Commitment of the Youthful Offender. *NPPA Journal*, 1956, 2 (2), 153–62.

Cavan, Ruth S. *Criminology, 3rd Ed.* New York: Crowell, 1962, 581–618.

Cavanogh, J. R. The effect of confinement on psychiatric patients. *United States Armed Forces Medical Journal*, 1951, 2, 1479–82.

Cavanogh, J. R. & Gerstein, S. Group psychotherapy in Naval disciplinary barracks. *United States Naval Medical Bulletin*, 1949, *49*, 645–49.

Cavanogh, J. R., Gerstein, S., Peters, E. R., & Mathew, T. J. Profile of a probation violator. *United States Armed Forces Medical Journal*, 1950, *1*, 1051–64.

Chappell, R. A. Naval offenders and their treatment. *Federal Probation*, 1945, *9* (2), 3–7.

Christensen, R. L. Character disorder: the twentieth century neurosis. *United States Armed Forces Medical Journal*, 1955, *6*, 1597–1604.

Cistola, F. V., Greenfield, R., & Teu, W. The prediction of AWOL. Privately circulated manuscript. Mental Hygiene Consultation Service, Ft. Leonard Wood, Missouri (undated).

Clark, J. H. The adjustment of Army AWOL's, *Journal of Abnormal and Social Psychology*, 1949, *44*, 394–401.

Claver, S. *Under The Lash: A History of Corporal Punishment in the British Armed Forces*. London: Torchstream, 1954.

Clemmer, D. *The Prison Community*. Boston: Christopher, 1940.

Clifton, T. D. Custody classification by consensus. *Military Police Journal*, 1962, *11* (8), 10–13.

Cloward, R. A. The role of the social worker under SR 210–185–1. In *Symposium on Military Social Work*. Washington: Social Services Branch Office of the Surgeon General, Department of the Army, 1952, pp. 98–100 (Mimeographed).

Cloward, R. A. Social control and anomie: A study of a prison community. (Doctoral dissertation, Columbia University) Ann Arbor, Michigan: University Microfilms, 1959, No. 59–2840.

Connelly, E. J. & Macalik, L. J. Group work services and the reception
process. Project *5–68*. The Council for Research, Evaluation and
Staff Development, U.S. Disciplinary Barracks, 1969.

Cook, R. A. Role of the psychologist in a United States Disciplinary
Barracks. Paper presented at the meeting of Army Clinical Psychologists, Washington, D.C., September, 1959.

Cook, R. A. Psychiatric assessment of military offenders. *Third Annual
Conference of United States Army Clinical Psychologists,* Office of
The Surgeon General, Department of The Army, Washington, D.C.,
1960.

Cooke, T. Soldiers, stockades, and psychiatry. *United States Armed Forces
Medical Journal,* 1959, *10,* 553–69.

Cornsweet, A. C., & Locke, B. Alcohol as a factor in Naval delinquencies.
United States Navy Medical Bulletin, 1946, *46,* 1690–95.

Couch, S. A. A statistical study of 247 short-term prisoners received at
USDB between 14 February 1963 and 31 March 1964. Project *2–64,*
Council for Research and Evaluation, United States Disciplinary
Barracks, 1964.

Coughlin, F. M. Army and Air Force Clemency and Parole Board—a brief
summary. *Security Police Digest,* 1968 (Summer), 16–17.

Datel, W. E. Socialization scale norms on military samples. *Military Medicine,* 1962, *127,* 740–44.

de Graaf, H. H. A. Outline of military criminal and disciplinary law in
the Netherlands. *Revue de Droit Penal Militaire et de Droit de la
Guerre,* 1965, *4* (1), 17–30.

De Hart, W. C. *Observations of Military Law and the Constitution and
Practice of Courts Martial.* New York: Appleton, 1862, 250–51.

De Smit, N. W. Aanpassingsproblematiek in de militaire situatie. *Maandbl.
geest. Volksgezonh,* 1964, *19* (3), 79–89.

Dienel, R. M. Social Work and The Military Offender. In *Collected Papers
from a Short Course on Current Trends in Army Social Work,* Washington, Walter Reed Army Institute of Research, 1960.

Dixon, R. C. Follow-up Study of Restorees. 3320th Retraining Group,
Amarillo Air Force Base, Texas, October 1963.

Dixon, R. C. *Follow-Up Study of Restorees of the 3320th Retraining
Group.* 3320th Retraining Group, Research and Analysis Division,
Amarillo Technical Training Center (ATC), Amarillo Air Force
Base, Texas, August 1965.

Dressler, D. Men on parole as soldiers in World War II. *Social Service
Review,* 1946, *20,* 537–50.

Dunn, W. H. The psychopath in the armed forces. *Psychiatry,* 1941, *4,*
251–59.

Erickson, M. Military injustice. *Playboy,* 1969 (June), 70–71.

Feldman, H. & Meleski, A. A. Factors Differentiating AWOL from Non-
AWOL Trainees. *Journal of Abnormal and Social Psychology,* 1948,
43, 70–77.

Ferencz, B. B. Rehabilitation of Army offenders. *Journal of Criminal Law and Criminology,* 1943, *34,* 245.

Force, R. C. Treatment of military offenders in a relatively permissive total environment. 3320th Retraining Group, Amarillo Air Force Base, Texas, 1954.

Force, R. C. Aptitudes and military delinquency. 3320th Retraining Group, Amarillo Air Force Base, Texas, 1958.

Force, R. C. & Meyers, J. K. Prediction of separation of Air Force trainees. *Journal of Psychological Studies,* 1959 *2,* 28–31.

Force, R. C. Handling military personnel who are non-effective due to a non-conformant behavior pattern. 3320th Retraining Group, Amarillo Air Force Base, Texas, 1961.

Force, R. C. The Air Force's new correctional treatment teams. 3320th Retraining Group, Amarillo Air Force Base, Texas, 1961.

Force, R. C. What are inmate needs for social education and how can they be determined? 3320th Retraining Group, Amarillo Air Force Base, Texas, September, 1961.

Force, R. C. Retrainees ego ideal. 3320th Retraining Group, Amarillo Air Force Base, Texas, January, 1963.

Freedman, H. L. & Rockmore, M. J. Marijuana, a factor in personality evaluation and Army maladjustment. *Journal of Clinical Psychopathology,* 1948, *8,* 221–36.

Futterman, E. H. Military offenses and juvenile delinquency: delinquency, parental attitudes and character formation of prisoners and other enlisted men in the Marine Corps. *Journal of Nervous and Mental Disorders,* 1963, *136,* 569–78.

Garber, W. F. The military delinquent. *Nervous Child,* 1955, *11,* 49–51.

Garetz, F. K. A follow-up study of first time military offenders. *Military Medicine,* 1961, *126,* 842–44.

Gatto, L. E. Understanding and management of the psychopath. *Air Surgeons News Letter,* 1952, No. 23, 8–21 (Supplemental Section).

Giffen, M. B. Forensic psychiatry USAF; further observations and considerations. *Military Medicine,* 1965, *130,* 55–59.

Giffen, M. B. & Kritzer, H. An aid to the psychiatrist in military forensic medicine. *Military Medicine,* 1961, *126,* 838–41.

Gibbs, J. C. Handling the military delinquent. *Army Information Digest,* 1961 (Feb.).

Glaser, Daniel. *The Effectiveness of a Prison and Parole System.* Bobbs-Merrill: Indianapolis, 1964.

Glasner, S. A psychiatric approach to the sociopathic patient. *Military Medicine,* 1966, *131,* 247–53.

Glass, A. J. & others. Psychiatric prediction and military effectiveness. Parts 1–2. *United States Armed Forces Medical Journal,* 1956, 7, 1427–43.

Glass, A. J. & others. Psychiatric prediction and military effectiveness. Part 3. Factors influencing psychiatrists. *United States Armed Forces Medical Journal,* 1957, *8,* 346–57.

Glenn, G. *The Army and the Law.* New York: AMS Press, 1943.

Goffman, E. *Asylums.* New York: Doubleday & Co., 1961.

Goldberg, H. L. Military psychiatric team. *Focus,* 1952, *31* (1) 12–17.

Goldberg, H. L., Hoefer, F. A. C. The Army parole system. *Journal of Criminal Law and Criminology,* 1949, *40,* 158–69.

Goodspeed, W. K. & others. The unsuitable enlisted seaman. *United States Armed Forces Medical Journal,* 1955, *6,* 244–48.

Gorham, W. A. A research study of the prediction of adaptability to the Navy. Psychological Research Associates, Washington, PRA report *56–9,* May, 1956.

Grabein, J. W., Tapogna, W. G., and Mooney, B. L. Study of differences between prisoners selected for the Special Training Program and prisoners in general. Project *1–64,* The Council for Research and Evaluation, United States Disciplinary Barracks, 1964.

Graff, N. Experiences in a prison hospital. *Bulletin of the Menninger Clinic,* 1956, *20,* 85–92.

Grant, J. D. Personality variables in military delinquency. Paper presented at the meeting of the American psychological Association, Cleveland, September, 1953.

Grant, J. D. A group dynamics approach to treating acting-out personalities. Paper presented at Clinical Psychology Research Conference of Bay Area Veterans Administration Facilities, Berkeley, November, 1953.

Grant, J. D. A report of the Camp Elliott rehabilitation research. Paper presented at Office of Naval Research sponsored meeting, Washington, D.C., February, 1957.

Grant, J. D. The use of correctional institutions as self-study communities in social research, *British Journal of Delinquency,* 1957, *7,* 301–8.

Grant, J. D. & Grant, M. Q. A group dynamics approach to the treatment of non-conformists in the Navy. *Annals of the American Academy of Political and Social Science,* 1959, *322,* 126–35.

Graves, B. C. Effectiveness of the MMPI test-retest in prediction of Air Force recidivism. Presented at the Regional Mental Health Clinic, Plainview, Texas, July, 1964.

Graves, B. C. Prediction of Air Force Recidivism by the MMPI test-retest. 3320th Retraining Group, Amarillo Air Force Base, Texas, June, 1963.

Gray, J. M. Evaluation of the Army's restoration program. Office of the Provost Marshall General, Department of the Army, Washington, D.C., 1964.

Guttmacher, M. G. & Stewart, F. A. A psychiatric study of absence without leave. *American Journal of Psychiatry,* 1945, *102,* 74–81.

Haas, A. & Kuras, E. J. Some antecedent factors in Army prisoners. *American Journal of Psychiatry,* 1958, *115,* 143–45.

Hadley, E. Military selection. *Psychiatry,* 1942, *5,* 371–400.

Hakeem, M. Armed forces and criminality. *Journal of Criminal Law and Criminology*, 1946, *37*, 120–31.

Halland, J. B. A balanced rehabilitation program for military offenders. *Military Review*, 1955, *35*, 52–54.

Hankoff, L. D. Rapid survey of delinquent servicemen. *United States Armed Forces Medical Journal*, 1958, *9*, 107–11.

Hankoff, L. D. Interaction patterns among military prison personnel. *United States Armed Forces Medical Journal*, 1959, *10*, 1416–27.

Hanley, C. An inventory of personal opinions. First technical report. San Diego: United States Naval Retraining Command, Camp Elliott, 1954.

Hannum, R. Problems of Getting Jobs for Parolees. *NPPA Journal* 1960, *6* (2).

Hart, R. F. Operational analysis of team treatment program. 3320th Retraining Group, Amarillo Air Force Base, Texas, September, 1964.

Hart, R. F. & Hippchen, L. J. Team treatment of Air Force Offenders. *American Journal of Correction*, 1966, *28* (5), 40–45.

Hedlund, J. L. Army Classification Scores: Their meaning and clinical interpretation. Paper prepared for the conference of Army Clinical Psychologists, Washington, D.C., September, 1959.

Heet, R. E. A history of the 3320th Retraining Group 1952–1962. 3320th Retraining Group, Amarillo Air Force Base, Texas, September, 1964.

√ Henderson, C. R. *Penal and Reformatory Institutions.* New York: Russell Sage Foundation, 1910, pp. 177–78.

Hippchen, L. J. Methodological problems in assessing ex-prisoners: Experiences of the 3320th Retraining Group. Presented at the annual meeting of the Southwestern Sociological Association, Dallas, Texas, April, 1962.

Hippchen, L. J. Attitudes of Amarillo area employers toward servicemen discharged under other than honorable conditions. 3320th Retraining Group, Amarillo Air Force Base, Texas, December, 1962.

Hippchen, L. J. The Air Force's operational therapeutic community concept in the treatment of selected military offenders. *American Journal of Correction*, 1963, *25* (1), 14–19.

Hippchen, L. J. Development of criteria for determining the restoration potentials of problem airmen. Preliminary Report No. 1. Behavioral Sciences Research Project, 3320th Retraining Group, Amarillo Air Force Base, Texas, July, 1964.

Hippchen, L. J. Analysis of organization structure in relationship to operational effectiveness of the 3320th Retraining Group. 3320th Retraining Group, Amarillo Air Force Base, Texas, January, 1965.

Hippchen, L. J. Some unique aspects of research in a therapeutic community. Presented at the Annual meeting of the Southwestern Sociological Association, Dallas, Texas, April, 1965.

Hippchen, L. J. Basis of an interaction approach in treatment of minor

offenders. Presented at the Fifth International Congress on Criminology, Montreal, Canada, August, 1965.

Hippchen, L. J., Dixon, R. C., & O'Donnell, R. D. Evaluation of the
retraining program. (A series of continuing six-month reports).
3320th Retraining Group, Amarillo Air Force Base, Texas, 1960–65.

Hippchen, L. J., Dixon, R. C., & O'Donnell, R. D. Descriptive characteristics of the 3320th Retraining Group and it's population, 1952–1961.
3320th Retraining Group, Amarillo Air Force Base, Texas, September, 1961 (1962, updated.)

Hippchen, L. J. & Dixon, R. C. Study of follow-up adjustment of restorees
for selected commands and bases. 3320th Retraining Group, Amarillo
Air Force Base, Texas, November, 1964.

Hippchen, L. J. & O'Donnell, R. D. Relationships of some important
sociological variables to restoration and discharge in the 3320th
Retraining Group. 3320th Retraining Group, Amarillo Air Force
Base, Texas, August, 1962.

Hirt, M. C. & Cook, R. A. Effectiveness of the California Psychological
inventory to predict psychiatric determinations of socialization.
Journal of Clinical Psychology, 1962, *18*, 176–77.

Hitchcock, J. Community psychiatry in a military setting. *Military Medicine*, 1965, *130*, 1198–1202.

Homans, G. C. *The Human Group*. New York: Harcourt, Brace & Co.,
1950.

Hoppe, A. Syndicated Column, *San Francisco Chronicle*, April 3, 1969.

Huie, W. B. *The Execution of Private Slovik*, Boston: Little, Brown, 1954.

Hymes, J. P. & Blackman, S. Situational variables in socially deviant behavior. *Journal of Social Psychology*, 1965, *65*, 149–53.

Illing, H. A. Some aspects of authority over groups of military offenders.
California Youth Authority, 1956, *9*, 27–30.

Information Section, 7th Logistical Compound, APO 47, San Francisco,
California. Progress in rehabilitation. *Military Police Journal*, 1962,
12 (3), 19.

Information Office, Ft. Leavenworth, Kansas. Military Training Branch
USDB salvages soldiers. *Military Police Journal*, 1962, *11*(6), 12–13.

Ireland, T. E. Article 15 and correctional custody. *Military Police Journal*,
1963, *12*(11), 14–15.

Isenstadt, P. M. Evaluation and recommendation of 5th Army stockade
training program. Project *6–67*, Council for Research and Evaluation, United States Disciplinary Barracks, 1967.

Ives, R. A. *A Treatise on Military Law and the Jurisdiction, Constitution,
and Procedure of Military Courts*. New York: Van Nostrand, 1879.

Ives, V. & others, Interpersonal variables related to recidivism in military
delinquency. *Rehabilitation Research*, United States Naval Retraining Command. Camp Elliott, San Diego, California.

Jacobson, E. Observations on psychological effect of imprisonment on
female political prisoners. In Eissler, K. R. (Ed.): *Searchlights on*

Delinquency. New York: International Universities Press, 1949, pp. 341–68.

Janowitz, M. *The Professional Soldier.* New York: Free Press, 1960.

Jenkins, I. What to do with AWOLs. *Combat Forces,* 1953, *4,* 42–44.

Johnson, E. H. *Crime, Correction and Society, revised edition.* Homewood, Illinois: Dorsey, 1968.

Jones, A. H. Study of disciplinary offenders in the United States Disciplinary Barracks. Project *1–63,* Council for Research and Evaluation, United States Disciplinary Barracks, 1963.

Jones, E. A survey of the pre-release program. Project *1–66,* Council for Research and Evaluation, United States Disciplinary Barracks, 1966.

Jourard, S. M. Identification, parent-cathexis, self-esteem. *Journal of Consulting Psychology,* 1957, *21,* 375–80.

Karanikas, D. T. Le service militaire et son influence sur la criminalite. *Annales Internationales Criminologie,* 1966, *2e,* 363–70.

Klieger, W. A., Dubuisson, A. U., and de Jung, J. E. Prediction of unacceptable performance in the Army. Army Human Factors Research Branch-Technical Research Note 113, June 1961.

Knapp, J. L. & Weitzen, F. A total psychotherapeutic push method as practiced in the 5th Service Command Rehabilitation Center, Ft. Knox, Ky. *American Journal of Psychiatry,* 1945, *102,* 362–66.

Knapp, R. R. Personality correlates of delinquency rate in a Navy sample. *Journal of Applied Psychology,* 1963, *47,* 68–71.

Knapp, R. R. Value and personality differences between offenders and non-offenders. *Journal of Applied Psychology,* 1964, *48,* 59–62.

Korson, S. M. The psychopath under stress in the military service. *Military Medicine,* 1955, *116,* 124–26.

Kramer, J. C. & Young, J. L. The psychiatrist as probation officer. *United States Armed Forces Medical Journal,* 1960, *11,* 454–58.

Krise, E. F. Role conflict and social diagnosis of the military offender. Unpublished doctoral dissertation, University of Chicago, June, 1958.

La Grone, C. W., Jr. Interrelationships among developmental characteristics of 500 military delinquents. *Journal of Clinical Psychology,* 1947, *3,* 330–41.

Larson, R. C. Punishment ends with the court-martial. *Army in Europe,* 1965 (August). Pp. 8–14.

Lawn, H. J. The Study and Treatment of Alcoholism in the 5th S.C. Rehabilitation Center. *American Journal of Psychiatry,* 1946, *102.*

Lejins, P. J. and Tanner, V. H. Military Careers of juvenile delinquents. *Proceedings of the 84th Annual Congress of Correction of the American Prison Association,* 1954. Pp. 223–39.

Loeser, L. The sexual psychopath in the military service. *American Journal of Psychiatry,* 1945, *102,* 92–101.

Levanthal, A. M. Character disorders, disciplinary offenders, and the MMPI. *United States Armed Forces Medical Journal,* 1960, *11,* 660–64.

Lewis, R. Procedure of military justice and disposition of military offenders. *Proceedings of the American Prison Association,* 1941. Pp. 107–20.

Linden, M. E. Relationship between social attitudes toward aging and the delinquents of youth. *American Journal of Psychiatry,* 1957, *114,* 444–48.

Litchfield, B. The Army's New Disciplinary Barracks. *Prison World,* 1948, *10* (3) 12–13, 30–31.

Locke, B. Comparison of Naval offenders with non-offenders on a projective sentence completion test. *United States Armed Forces Medical Journal,* 1957, *8,* 1825–28.

Locke, B. & Cornsweet, A. C. Naval personal inventory and Naval offender. *United States Navy Medical Bulletin,* 1949, *49,* 289–95.

Locke, B., Cornsweet, A. C., Bromberg, W., & Apuzzo, A. A. Study of 1063 Naval Offenders. *United States Navy Medical Bulletin,* 1945, *44,* 73–86.

Lubetsky, J., Kisel, J. G., & Blume, R. M. An exploratory evaluation of a Mental Hygiene Consultation Service field program. *Military Medicine,* 1963, *128,* 1212–16.

Lyon, W. B. Character and behavior disorders. *Military Medicine,* 1964, *129,* 355–63.

Lyon, W. B. The relationship of background factors to initial adjustment in the Navy. *American Psychologist,* 1965, *20,* 593.

Lyon, W. B. The etiology of various character and behavior disorders. Paper presented at the meeting of the Southeastern Psychological Association, New Orleans, Louisiana, April, 1966.

Lyon, W. B. Some thoughts on juvenile delinquency and the Navy. Privately circulated paper, 1966.

MacCormick, A. H. Some basic considerations in the discipline of military prisoners. *Federal Probation,* 1945, *9* (1).

MacCormick, A. H. and Enjen, V. The Army's postwar program for military prisoners. *Prison World,* 1947, *9* (3), 3–7, 32–35, 38.

Maglin, W. H. Rehabilitation, The keynote of the Army's correctional program. *Federal Probation,* 1955, *19* (2) 21–28.

Martin, C. V. Treatment of character and behavior disorders in the military. *Corrective Psychiatry and Journal of Social Therapy,* 1965, *11,* 163–67.

Mattick, H. W. Parolees in the Army during World War II. *Federal Probation,* 1960, *24* (3), 49–55.

Maynard, P. E. USDB vocational industries building on the way. *Military Police Journal,* 1964, *12* (9), 10.

McCartney, J. L. & Cusick, F. J. Classifications of prisoners in American civil and military correctional institutions. *Military Medicine,* 1959, *124,* 447–52.

McCorkle, L. W. & Korn, R. Resocialization within walls. In Johnson, N.,

Savitz, L., & Wolfgang, M. E. (Eds.), *The Sociology of Punishment and Corrections.* New York: Wiley, 1962.

McSally, F. Finding Jobs for Released Offenders. *Federal Probation,* 1960, *24* (2).

Melichercik, J. Employment Problems of Former Offenders. *NPPA Journal,* 1956, *2*, 43.

Menninger, W. C. Psychiatry and the military offender. *Federal Probation,* 1945, *9* (2).

Menninger, W. C. & Berlion, I. C. Psychiatric aspects of the problem of clemency in military corrections. *Prison World,* 1945, *7*(4), 27–29.

Milgram, S. Behavioral study of obedience. *Journal of Abnormal and Social Psychology,* 1963, *67*, 371–78.

Miller, P. R. The prison code. *American Journal of Psychiatry,* 1958, *114*, 583–85.

Monahan, F. T. Problem soldier rehabilitation through mental hygiene consultation service. *Infantry Journal,* 1962 (January–February).

Mooney, B. L. Characteristics of restorees. Project *4–64,* Council for Research and Evaluation, U.S. Disciplinary Barracks, 1964.

Mooney, B. L. and Jones, R. L., Jr. Design, SOP, Administrative Procedures, and staff responsibilities for follow-up study of former USDB inmates. Privately circulated manuscript, U.S. Disciplinary Barracks, 1963.

Murphy, D. B. & Langston, R. D. A short form of the Wechsler-Bellvue and the Army Classification Battery as measures of intelligence. *Journal of Consulting Psychology,* 1956, *20*, 405.

Murphy, J. M. & Grant, J. D. The role of psychiatry in Naval retraining. *United States Armed Forces Medical Journal,* 1952, *3*, 631–34.

Mutual Welfare News, Mutual Welfare League, Naval Prison, Portsmouth, N.H., Sept. 14, 1919.

Newman, C. A study of the relationship between attitudes toward certain authority figures and adjustment to the military service. (Doctoral dissertation, New York University) Ann Arbor, Michigan: University Microfilms, 1954, No. 54–3577.

Nichols, J. D. Follow-up study of men receiving certificates of accomplishment for vocational and other training. Projects *3–62, 3–64,* and *3–66,* Council for research and evaluation, United States Disciplinary Barracks, 1962, 1964, and 1966.

Nichols, J. D. & Brodsky, S. L. After they leave: A vocational follow-up study of former prisoners. *American Journal of Corrections,* 1967, *29* (3), 27–30.

Nichols, R. S. The ineffective soldier: Research and policy problems. Paper presented at the meeting of the American Psychological Association, New York, September, 1961.

Nichols, R. S. First court-martial screening program pilot study. Project *6X–97–87–001,* Mental Hygiene Consultation Service, Fort Bragg, N.C., 1962.

O'Callahan vs. Parker. *Criminal Law Reporter,* 1038 (1969); and 5 *Criminal Law Reporter,* 3082 (1969).

O'Donnell, R. D. Third annual research program status report. 3320th Retraining Group, Amarillo Air Force Base, Texas, June, 1963.

O'Neal, B. Development of criteria for determining the restoration potentials of problem airmen. Preliminary report No. 2, 3320th Retraining Group, Amarillo Air Force Base, Texas, 1965.

Oje, C. V. The Air Force corrections and retraining program. *Federal Probation Quarterly,* 1955, *19,* 31–38.

Paul, L. H. Counseling the youthful offender. *Military Police Journal,* 1964, *14* (3), 20–21.

Performance study of prisoners restored to duty during the period, 1 January 1958, through 31 December 1958 (and subsequent studies published annually). Bureau of Naval Personnel, Department of the Navy, Washington, D.C., 1959.

Perl, W. R. Military delinquency and service motivation. *Military Review,* 1954, *33,* 21–27.

Perlman, Helen H. The role concept and social casework: some explorations. I. The "social" in social casework. *Social Service Review,* 1961, *35,* 374–75.

Pierce, C. M. The recruit prisoner. *Military Medicine,* 1959, *124,* 131–40.

Plag, J. A. The practical value of a psychiatric screening interview in predicting military ineffectiveness. Report *64–7,* United States Navy Medical Neuropsychiatric Research Unit, San Diego, California, 1964.

Plag, J. A. & Arthur, R. J. Psychiatric re-examination of unsuitable Naval recruits: a two-year follow-up. *American Journal of Psychiatry,* 1965, *122,* 534–41.

Plan for the Establishment and Operation of the Air Force Retraining Center. Headquarters USAF, the Inspector General, The Air Provost Marshal, Washington, D.C. August, 1951.

Powelson, H. and Bendix, R. Psychiatry in prison. *Psychiatry,* 1951, *14,* 73–86.

Quinn, D. Salvage or Scrap? *Military Police Journal,* 1965, *14* (11), 12–16.

Quinn, D. Consider the turtle. *Military Police Journal,* 1966, *15* (11), 5–8.

Ramsey, R. R. The Army's new correctional program at stockade level. *Federal Probation,* 1959, *23* (3), 41–43.

Ramsey, R. R. Military offenders and the Army correctional program. In Bloch, H. A. (Ed.), *Crime in America.* Philosophical Library, New York, 1961.

Rashkis, H. A. Notes on interviewing AWOL soldiers. *Journal of Abnormal and Social Psychology,* 1945, *40,* 100–101.

Regnier, A. J. A practical solution to the AWOL problem. *Military Review,* 1955, *35,* 45–51.

Research Report: Evaluation of the Retraining Group. Semi-Annual Report from May 1962. 3320th Retraining Group, Amarillo Air Force Base, Texas and Lowry Air Force Base, Colorado.

Richardson, R. E. Conserving human resources. *Army Information Digest,* 1963, *35,* 45–51.

Roff, M. Pre-service personality problems and subsequent adjustments of military service. 1. Gross outcome in relation to acceptance-rejection at induction and military service. USAF School of Aviation Medicine, Randolph Field, Texas. April, 1956, *55–138,* 17p.

Roos, C. & Barry, J. *Bibliography of Military Psychiatry: 1952–1958.* Washington, D.C.: National Library of Medicine, H.E.W., 1959.

Rubio, M. Psychopathologic reaction patterns in the Antilles command. *United States Armed Forces Medical Journal,* 1955, *6,* 1767–72.

Rushton, M. The Army's new correctional division. *Prison World,* 1944, *6* (6), 4–6.

Ryan, F. J. *The relation of performance to social background factors among Army inductees.* Washington, D.C.: Catholic University of America Press, 1958.

Schlessinger, N. & Blau, D. A. psychiatric study of retraining command. *United States Armed Forces Medical Journal,* 1957, *8,* 397–405.

Schlotterback, D. L. The USDB group orientation and counseling program. Project *2–62,* Council for Research and Evaluation, United States Disciplinary Barracks, 1962.

Schneider, A. J. N., La Grone, C. W., Jr., Glueck, E. T., & Glueck, S. Prediction of behavior of civilian delinquents in the Armed Forces. *Mental Hygiene,* 1944, *28* (3), 1–20.

Schneider, A. J. N. & La Grone, C. W. Delinquents in the Army: a statistical study of 500 rehabilitation center prisoners. *American Journal of Psychiatry,* 1945, *102,* 82–91.

Selling, L. Some problems of the anti-social ex-serviceman. *Federal Probation,* 1945, *8* (2), 22–26.

Sellman, W. S. A study of the relationship of incidents and restoration in the 3320th Retraining Group. 3320th Retraining Group, Amarillo Air Force Base, Texas, November, 1964.

Sellman, W. S. Social education in the 3320th Retraining Group. 3320th Retraining Group, Amarillo Air Force Base, Texas, April, 1965.

Shackleford, D. The youthful offender and the armed forces. *NPPA Journal,* 1958, *4* (2), 148–55.

Shainberg, D. Personality restriction in adolescents. *Psychiatric Quarterly,* 1966, *40,* 258–70.

Shainberg, D. Motivations of adolescent military offenders. *Adolescence,* 1967, *2,* 243–54.

Shainberg, D. & Symonds, M. Some thoughts on the sense of self in military offenders. Paper presented at the meeting of the American Psychiatric Association, New York, May, 1965.

Shattuck, E. Military service for men with criminal records. *Federal Probation,* 1945, *9* (1), 12–14.

Shaw, C. C. & Singer, R. C. The brig medical officer. *Military Medicine.* 1958, *122*, 108–13.

Sherman, M. H. The immaturity reaction in military service. *Psychoanalysis,* 1954, *2*, 38–47.

Shulman, B. H. Group psychotherapy in a post stockade. *Journal of Social Therapy,* 1957, *3*, 14–18.

Simon, R. M. The stockade revisited: Psychiatry in a screening program. *Military Medicine,* 1965, *130*, 980–85.

Simons, R. C. The stockade sentry: Two case reports. *Military Medicine,* 1963, *128*, 1005–10.

Singer, R. G. Evaluation of amnesia in brig medical practice. *United States Armed Forces Medical Journal,* 1958, *9,* 21–28.

Singer, R. G. & Shaw, C. C. The passive-aggressive personality. *United States Armed Forces Medical Journal,* 1957, *8,* 62–69.

Skinner, Emmett W. The Navy's correctional program. *Prison World,* 1945, *7,* 8–9 & 27–30.

Skobba, J. Review of progress in military psychiatry. *American Journal of Psychiatry,* 1960, *116,* 561.

Sollito, B. J. A case for cooperation! Delinquency control. *Military Police Journal,* 1964, *13* (11), 7–10.

Spencer, J. C. *Crime and the Services.* London: Routledge and Kegan Paul, 1954.

State of New York Department of Corrections. Characteristics of inmates discharged from New York State Correctional Institutions, 1963. Albany, N.Y., 1964.

Stoller, R. J. & Geerstma, R. H. The consistency of psychiatrists' judgments. *Journal of Nervous and Mental Disease,* 1963, *137,* 58–66.

Stouffer, G. A. & Otness, H. R. 100 civilian delinquents in the Navy. *Journal of Clinical Psychopathology,* 1946, *8,* 251–70.

Street, D. The inmate group in custodial and treatment settings. *American Sociological Review,* 1965, *30,* 40–65.

Sullivan, C. E. Delinquency integrations. *Rehabilitation Research,* United States Naval Retraining Command, Camp Elliott, San Diego, California, 38p.

Sunderland, J. O. Social work in an Army Disciplinary Barracks. In *Symposium on Military Social Work.* Washington: Social Service Branch, Office of the Surgeon General, Department of the Army, 1952, pp. 94–97. (Mimeographed)

Sutherland, E. H.: *Principles of Criminology.* Philadelphia: J. Lippincott, 1947.

Taft, D. R. *Criminology 3rd Ed.* New York: Macmillan, 1956, 748–53.

Tappan, P. W. *Crime, Justice, and Corrections.* New York: McGraw-Hill, 1960, 749.

Thorne, F. C. The frustration-anger-hostility states: a new diagnostic classification. *Journal of Clinical Psychology,* 1953, *9,* 334–39.

Thorne, F. C. Epidemiological studies of chronic frustration-hostility-aggression states. *American Journal of Psychiatry*, 1957, *113*, 717–21.

Thurrell, R. J., Halleck, S. L., & Johnsen, A. F. Psychosis in prison. *Journal of Criminal Law, Criminology, and Police Science*, 1965, *56*, 271–76.

Tolpin, P. H. Psychiatric evaluation of military prisoners. *United States Armed Forces Medical Journal*, 1953, *4*, 883–87.

Trenaman, J. *Out of Step*. New York: Philosophical Library, 1952.

Turner, C. C. Restoring the military prisoner: The man with a past also has a future. *Army Information Digest*, 1965, *20*, 57–61.

USAF prisoner retraining program. *Air Force Pamphlets 125-2-1*, Department of the Air Force, 16 May 1960.

USAF Prisoner Retraining Program, TIG Brief, 1962, *14*, 21.

Von Holden, M. H. Analysis of attitudes expressed by prisoners leaving the U.S. Disciplinary Barracks. Project *8–67*, Council for Research, Evaluation and Staff Development, U.S. Disciplinary Barracks, 1968.

Von Holden, M. H. & Kroll, J. L. Restoration success: a follow up study. Project *17–67*, Council for Research, Evaluation, and Staff Development, U.S. Disciplinary Barracks, 1968.

Von Holden, M. H. & Isenstadt, P. I. A study of MOS description titles for guards. U.S. Disciplinary Barracks, 1969.

Wagley, P. Some criminologic implications of the returning soldier. *Journal of Criminal Law and Criminology*, 1944, *34*, 311–14.

West, L. J. An approach to the problem of homosexuality in the military service. *American Journal of Psychiatry*, 1958, *115*, 392–401.

Westmoreland, W. W. Mental Health—an aspect of command, *Military Medicine*, 1963. *128*, 209–14.

Wiedenfeld, James I. Research Report: Annual Trend Analysis of *Retrainee Population*. Research and Analysis Division, 3320th Retraining Group, Amarillo Air Force Base, Texas, September 1965.

Wiener, F. B. *Civilians Under Military Justice*. Chicago: University of Chicago Press, 1967.

Williams, J. N. The sub-standard mentally and abnormal behavior pattern serviceman. *Military Medicine*, 1958, *123*, 48–52.

Wise, R. E. Public Employment of Persons with a Criminal Record. *NPPA Journal*, 1960, *6* (2).

Witmer, H. and others. Men unadapted to military service. *Smith College Studies*, 1943, *13*, 299–336.

Wright, E. A. Soldiers in trouble. *Army*, 1965, *15*, 35–37.

Zald, M. N. The correctional institution for juvenile offenders: An analysis of organizational character. *Social Problems*, 1960, *8* (1), 65.

INDEX

Adjustment Board: Air Force, 78
Alabama: follow-up of prisoners from, 12
Alcoholics Anonymous: in USDB, 154, 156
Alcoholism, 61, 67
Amarillo Air Force Base (3320th Retraining Group): history, 20, 76–77, 112–16; description, 20–21, 77; number of prisoners, 76; mission, 76; multi-disciplinary approach, 76; follow-up after discharge, 76–77, 112–16; treatment program, 77, 83–85, 86; organization, 80–81; Operations and Training Division, 80, 82, 83; Supervisory Division, 80, 82, 84; Educational Services Division, 80, 82, 83; Analysis Division, 80, 85–86; Treatment Teams, 81–83, 86; phases of program, 83–85. *See also* Policy, Air Force Correctional
American Red Cross: aid in evaluation, 70
Army and Air Force Clemency Board, 17
Arson, 79
Auto Mechanics trade: at USDB, 159
AWOL: research on, 8; action by commanding officer, 10; rate at Ft. Dix, 72

Barber training: at USDB, 159
Brig: description of, 15, 48–49; codes in, 47–50, 53; research on, 48–49; personnel pattern, 48–51; formal program, 48, 54–55; Manual, 48; complaints in, 50, 52

British Correctional program: during World War II, 25; restoration in, 25, 26; like U.S. Air Force program, 26
British criminals: punishment, 4; parolees studied, 8, 11
Bunche, Richard, Private: killed at Presidio stockade, 7

Camp Elliott: restoration training at, 20; program, 20; research on organization and staff, 20; use of program in California, 21; research on role perceptions, 20, 22
Carpentry: training for trade in, 160
Classification: Army and Air Force Clemency Board, 17; for parole at USDB, 17; annual review of, at USDB, 17; in Air Force corrections, 21; and rehabilitation, 64; custody and, at Ft. Dix, 71, 72; functions performed by treatment teams, 81, 84; clinical evaluation for, 91; decision process, 91–97. *See also* Clemency; Parole; Restoration to duty, Security
Classification Board: at Ft. Dix, 65, 69, 70–71; Air Force, 84
Clemency: reduction in sentence, 17; change of discharge, 17; restoration to duty, 17; "Christmas," 31; social work evaluation for, 69; Air Force, 84; Mental Hygiene evaluation for, 91; decision process, 91; Mental Hygiene research on, 95–97. *See also* Classification; Parole; Restoration to duty; Security

Clemency Board: **Army and Air Force,** 17; at Ft. Dix, 63, 65–66, 69, 70–71

Clothing trades: training for, at USDB, 160

College: courses, at USDB, 154, 156

Combat: as a constraint for kindness, 38

Command and Staff College, Ft. Leavenworth, Kansas, 17

Communication: authoritarian, 16; in stockades, 16; between industry and corrections, 21; interaction patterns, 45–69; freedom of, 46; penal attitudes toward, 46, 47; psychiatrist's need for, 46–47; codes about, 46, 47, 49, 52, 54; custodial officers' patterns of, 47; in brig, 49, 52, 54, 55; in Air Force Retraining Group, 86

Congress: and first military prison, 15

Conscientious objector, 7

Correctional Training Facility, Ft. Riley, Kansas: description, 18; first-year results, 18; counseling in, 18

Counseling: positive group techniques in, 5; at Correctional Training Facility, 18; at Portsmouth Navy Prison, 19; at Camp Elliott, 20: at Amarillo Retraining Command, 21, 80–86 *passim*, 170; and punishment, 40; and Mental Hygiene, 40; at Ft. Dix stockade, 61, 66, 73; at USDB, 61; about discipline, 78; program rated at USDB, 153, 155; about employment, 170

Court martial: rate, at Ft. Dix, 73

Criminals, civilian: problems in research about, 7–8; joining the military services, 7–8, 9, 10; and military offenses, 7–9; studied in service, 8; parolees in service, 8; Navy research on 8, 9; and the draft, 9; caused by military service, 9–11; assisted by military service, 12–14

Culture of Correctional Institutions: prisonization, 38, 41; prisoner's advice on rehabilitation, 40; for psychiatrist, 46; codes, 46, 47; of prisoners, 46, 47; for guards, 46, 47; about communication, 46, 49, 52, 54; brig

interaction patterns, 46–59; and rehabilitation, 47; studied with discussion group, 48; organizational factors in, 49–58; and the spokesman, 57

Custody: maximum, at USDB, 7; minimum, at USDB, 17; minimum, at Ft. Dix, 65. See also Security

Dale Carnegie program: in USDB, 154, 156

Dependents: jurisdiction of military over, 5

Discharge: types, 10; changed, 17; effect on restoration to duty, 26; recommended, 60, 71; at Ft. Dix, 64–65, 66, 71; from Air Force, 78, 84; research on, 92–93, 94

Discharged servicemen: jurisdiction of military over, 5

Discipline: in Roman Legion, 3; and deterrence, 4; and punishment as an example, 4; positive type, 4–5; issues debated, 5; and group relations, 5; Supreme Court comments on, 6; as a cause of violations, 11; in Navy prisons, 19; in World War II, 19; publicity about, 33; reward and punishment and, 34; Character Guidance and, 34; in brig, 51–54, 55, 56; and Ft. Dix staff, 67, 71, 72; in Air Force, 78. See also Punishment

Draft: and offenses, 9; screening and, 10,12; in World War II, 13

Durham Rule, 145

Education: Air Force Retraining Group, 80, 82, 83; at USDB, rated, 153–57; High School GED program, 154, 156

Electrician trade: training for, at USDB, 160

Employment: of prisoners by staff, 67; Air Force training for, 84; USDB vocational training research, 85–86, 152–58, 159–63; and restorees, 98–

105; pre-release counseling for, 154, 156; USDB prisoners' preferences, 154, 156–57; post-discharge, 165; Air Force counseling about, 170–80 *passim;* Air Force survey of employers about, 170–80. *See also* Vocational Training
Enlistment: motives, 8–9

Farm: USDB, 17, 154, 156
First offenses, 11, 14
Ft. Dix Stockade: inattention by Post Commanders, 60; 1954 problems in, 61; characteristics of prisoners in, 61; policy in, 64; Mental Hygiene procedures in, 65, 68–74; Mental Hygiene role in, 66, 68–70, 73; rehabilitative programs in, 67; referrals to Mental Hygiene from, 67, 73
Ft. Leavenworth, Kansas. *See* United States Disciplinary Barracks

General Educational Development test (GED), 154, 156
Group Therapy: at Camp Elliott, 20; in Air Force Group, 22, 81–83; in the brig, 57; at the USDB, 154, 156
Guards: displacing anger, 16, 22, 54; at USDB, 17; replaced by prisoners in Navy prison, 18; research on, in brigs, 22; modeling, 22; Camp Elliott research on, 22; role with Mental Hygiene, 22, 47, 68; Mental Hygiene screening of, 22, 58; Ft. Dix research on, 22, 65, 67, 71, 72; USDB prisoners' perceptions of, 22, 134–39; culture in brig, 46–47, 53; relationships with staff, 47, 53, 54, 55; attitudes toward prisoners, 51–53, 56; handling of prisoners, 51–54, 55–56; as group leaders, 53; personality characteristics, 57–58; in Air Force, 79–80, 82, 84. *See also* Punishment; Security; Staff

Homosexuals, 61, 67
Honolulu, 5
Honor barracks, USDB, 17
Honor Company, Navy, 19

Illinois prisons: research, 12
Individual therapy: 14; rated by USDB prisoners, 154, 156
Insanity: mental status examination for, 93; definition, 145; in prisoners, 145; in Wisconsin prisoners, 145; Mental Hygiene evaluation of, 145, 146–48

Jail: City and County like stockade, 6
Jurisdiction of military courts: over dependents, 5; over discharged servicemen, 5
Juvenile delinquents: in the military, 8

Lackland Air Force Base, Texas: stockade, 15–16
Laundry: USDB training for employment in, 160
Length of confinement: Air Force prisoners, 78, 85
Letters: prisoner's control of, 18
London: vocational research on prisoners, 152
Lowry Air Force Base, Colorado: restoration program, 20; description, 20. *See* Amarillo Air Force Base

Machinist trade: training for employment in, at USDB, 159
Malingerer: deterrence, 38; in the brig, 56
Mental Hygiene: treatment for prisoners with military offenses only, 14; unit consultation, 14; role of psychiatrist in, 46, 47, 48, 70–71; evaluating prisoners in stockade, 58, 61, 71–74; psychotherapy, 66; handling

special problems, 66, 73; functions at Ft. Dix, 68, 73; social work program, 69–70, 145–46; procedures at Ft. Dix, 70; evaluation of prisoners, 78, 145–48; in Air Force Retraining Group, 80–83; in Air Force treatment teams, 81–83, 86; Air Force treatment program, 83–85; Air Force treatment results, 85–86; mental status examination, 93; research on role perceptions in USDB, 131–44; research on diagnosis, USDB, 145–48; research on mental ability, USDB, 148–51. *See also* Guards; Rehabilitation; Staff

Mental status examination, 93

Mess hall: training for employment in, at USDB, 160

Military Justice: laws, 5; composition of courts, 5; jurisdiction, 5; Uniform Code of Military Justice, 5; Supreme Court decisions about, 5, 6; system, 5–7; procedures, 5–8 *passim;* publicity about, 7; local punishment and court martial, 10; for first offenses, 11; for military offenses, 11; and recidivism, 61, 62, 67, 73; pre-trial sanity determinations, 70, 93; Ft. Dix Court Martial rates, 73; Air Force courts martial, 78

Military Training Program, 17, 18, 98, 154, 156

MMPI, 146

Murder: penalty for, 4; in Air Force, 79

Mutiny, 7

Mutual Welfare League: Thomas Osborne and, 18; policy, 18; history, 18

Narcotics, 61–67, 78, 79 *passim*

News: reporting of, 18

New York, research on insanity in prisoners, 145

O'Callahan: Supreme Court decision on, 5–6

Offenses: first, 11; Army prisoners', 60–61, 67, 72, 73, 100, 104, 105, 109; at Amarillo AFB, 76, 78, 79

Osborne, Thomas, 18

Parker: Supreme Court decision on, 5–6

Parole: civilian parolees in the military, 8, 12; from Illinois prisons, 12; success rates, 13; at USDB, 17; at Ft. Dix, 63, 66, 69, 70–71; Clemency Board, 65–66, 69, 70–71; Mental Hygiene evaluation for, 66, 68, 69, 91; decision process for, 91; Mental Hygiene research on, 95–97

Penitentiaries: vocational research in, 152

Personality: and prisoners' response to punishment, 52, 56–57, 58; of prisoners, 58, 61, 78, 98–105, 145, 146; prisoners provoking hostility, 61–62; identification of prisoners, 63–64; psychiatric evaluation of prisoners, 145–46, 147, 148; mental ability of prisoners, 148–51

Plumbing trade: USDB training for, 160

Policy, Air Force Correctional: and Clemency Board, 17; on restorable prisoners and USDB, 17, 20; crime rate and, 20; implications from research, 21; Air Provost Marshal's recommendations, 1947, 76; mission, 76; assumptions about prisoners, 76; rehabilitation goal, 76; multidisciplinary approach, 76; therapeutic community, 76; command control, 77; prisoner screening boards, 78; courts martial, 78; organization of program, 80–81

Policy, Army Correctional: history, 15; rationale, 15; on restoration to duty, 17, 19, 23–25, 26, 91–95, 98–105, 106, 128, 113–14, 114–16; staffing, 21–22; pressures on, 28; product of compromise, 28; leadership, 28, 30; agencies involved, 28, 30; goal confusion in, 29, 32; requirements, 31–33; objectives, 33–34, 34–37; economic considerations, 37, 38; constraints, 37–39; goal conflict, 39–41; reformation, 41; current goals, 41–43; recommendations, 44–45; system approach, 44–45; at Ft. Dix stockade, 64; trends, 106, 110; in World War II, 112; in Korean War, 113–14; post-Korean War, 114–16

Policy, Navy Correctional: use of Portsmouth Navy Prison, 19; discipline, 19; in World War II, 19; on restoration to duty, 20; on punishment, 29; general, 106, 110

Portsmouth Naval Prison, New Hampshire: established, 18; names of, 18; Thomas Osborne at, 18; Mutual Welfare League, 18; prisoner self-government at, 18; population of, 18–19; description of, 19; honor company in, 19; discipline, 19; counseling, 19, 40; restoration to duty from, 19, 20, 112–16, 125–26; in World War II, 19, 112; punishment in, 56

Presidio, at San Francisco, 7

Pre-trial sanity determination: at Ft. Dix, 70

Printing trade; USDB training for, 159

Prisoners: role of, 6; population screening, 8, 9, 10–11, 61, 78; acting as guards, 18; Navy honor company, 19; in World War II in Portsmouth, 19; from combat zones, 38–39; relationships with staff, 40, 62–63, 131–44; brig, evaluated by Mental Hygiene, 57; psychiatric evaluation of, 58, 61, 65–73 *passim*, 93, 145–48; at Ft. Dix, 60–75; resistance to rehabilitation, 62–63, 64; amenable to rehabilitation, 63, 64; number, at Amarillo, 76; characteristics of Air Force, 78–80; life history variables, 100; perceptions of roles, 131–44; USDB characteristics, 133; ratings of USDB programs, 152–58

Protest: in Army stockade, 7

Psychiatry. *See* Mental Hygiene

Psychology. *See* Mental Hygiene

Psychotherapy: at Ft. Dix, 66; research on, 154, 156

Punishment: and deterrence, 3–5, 29; by King Richard I, 4; described, 4; replaced by other approaches, 4–5; other than confinement, 10; in World War II, 19; meaning discussed, 28; reward-punishment approach, 34; for combat cases, 38–39; and counseling, 40; conflicts with rehabilitation, 40–41; against policy, 41; disguised as security, 42, 44; as a constraint, 43; in brigs, 51–54, 55–57; prisoners' response to, 52, 56–57, 58, 68; mass, 53, 57; as a homeostatic function, 55; at Ft. Dix, 65, 67, 68, 71, 72; in Air Force Retraining Group, 78

Quarles: Supreme Court decision, 5–6

Radio-TV repair: USDB training for employment in, 159

Rape, 79

Rebellion: at Presidio, 7; at Ft. Dix, 61, 66

Recidivism: at Ft. Dix, 61, 62, 67, 73

Recreation program: at USDB, 154, 156

Referrals: to Mental Hygiene, 75

Rehabilitation: through induction, 7, 9, 10, 11, 12, 14; psychological base for, 13, 15; for character and behavior disorder, 14; at USDB, 17, 18, 34, 36, 61, 91–95, 98–105, 113–16; semantics in, 29; ignored, 29, 30; as a goal, 29, 98; program, 34; stockade program for, 36, 42, 65–67, 69, 70–71; versus economy, 40; versus deterrence, 40; and punishment, 40–41; stockade research, 42, 65–67; as a constraint, 43; required research, 44; and culture, 47; prisoner resistance to, 62–63, 64; susceptibility to, 62–63; role of stockade personnel, 67–68; measurement at Ft. Dix, 71–

75; at Amarillo Retraining Group,
76–77, 86–87; expected at USDB,
133
Religious program: in USDB, rated,
154, 156
Requests, special: Mental Hygiene
handling of, 69
Research Council: at USDB, 18, 98–
105, 113–16, 141–44, 152–58
Restoration to duty: reformation by,
8; Navy research on, 12–13; Mental
Hygiene activity in, 14; socialization
by, 14–15; selective factors in, 14,
18, 98–105, 108; at USDB, 17; military training for, 17, 18, 154, 156;
at Correctional Training Facility,
18; in Navy prison, 19–20; in Navy
after World War II, 20; in Lowry
Air Force Base, 20; in Air Force
Retraining Group, 20, 76, 77, 84–87
passim, 112–16, 122–25; description
of process, 23, 91–97; significance of,
23–25; and social distance, 24; as a
goal, 24; difference from civilian
prisons, 24–25; British experience,
25–26; effect of discharge on, 26;
Air Force success rate in, 26; Army
success rate, 26; at Ft. Dix, 64, 65,
70–71, 73–74; Air Force research on,
85–86, 91–95, 98, 99, 122–25; policies, 106–10; in World War II, 112;
rates, 112–16; evaluation of program, 122–25, 125–26
Richard I, King of England: punishment of offenders, 4
Rock Island Arsenal, Illinois, 15
Role perceptions: in therapeutic institutions, 131; in juvenile institutions, 131; and social relationships,
131; in USDB, 131–44; and prison
role, 132, 134–39; and rank, 132,
139; and length of stay in institution, 132, 139–140
Roman Legion: discipline, 3–5

San Francisco: Army stockade, Presidio, 7

Screening Boards: Ft. Dix, 61; Air
Force, 78
Screening prisoners, 8, 9, 10–11, 61,
64–66, 78
Secretary of War: and USDB, 15
Security: maximum, at USDB, 17;
minimum, at USDB, 17; in Navy
prison, 17; required in corrections,
34; as a constraint on program, 36–
37, 43; conflicts with rehabilitation,
41; effectiveness, 42; research on,
42–44; discussion, 44, 53; in a brig,
55; in Ft. Dix stockade, 61, 62, 65–
66, 67, 69, 70–71, 72–73, 79–80; risks,
62, 67; minimum, at Ft. Dix, 65; in
Air Force Retraining Group, 77–78,
79–80, 84; Air Force Adjustment
Board and, 78. See also Custody;
Guards; Prisoners; Punishment
Sentence, Prisoners': in Air Force, 78
Sentence Completion Test, 146
Sheet metal training: at USDB, 159
Shoe repair training: at USDB, 159
Sick call: rate at Ft. Dix, 71–72
Slovik, Eddie D., Private: executed, 4
Social histories, 93
Social work: in stockades, 69–70, 71,
91–93, 145–46
Staff: in stockades, 16; unqualified,
16; as disciplinarians, 16; at USDB,
described, 17, 21–22; research on
supervisors, 20, 131–40; in Air Force
Group, 21, 77, 80, 81, 82; research
on, 21, 80, 85–86; treatment teams,
21, 81–83; guards, 22, 48–59 passim;
Ft. Dix research on, 22–23; rehabilitative relationships, 40; in brigs,
48–59; evaluation by Mental Hygiene, 58, 68–73; relationships with
prisoners, 62–63, 67, 68, 71, 72; in
stockades, 64–67; professional relationships, 68; social work, 69–70,
145–46; Air Force Retraining Group
organization of, 77, 80, 81, 82; treatment program in Air Force, 83–85,
86; role perception of, 132, 134–39.
See also Guards; Mental Hygiene;
Rehabilitation

Stockades: size, 6; purpose, 6; compared to civilian jails, 6; criticized, 7; joint Army-Air Force operation, 15–16; as a holding facility, 16; bad image as a deterrent, 16; problems in, 16; staffing in, 16; research on, 16, 48, 71–74; problem of local control, 16, 60; Mental Hygiene evaluation in, 58, 61, 71–74; population characteristics, 61; Mental Hygiene cooperation, 66, 68–74. *See also* Brig; Ft. Dix Stockade; Lackland Air Force Base, Texas; Presidio

Supreme Court: decision on *Toth* v. *Quarles*, 5–6; decision on *O'Callahan* v. *Parker*, 5–6; decision questioned, 6; comments on discipline from, 6

Therapeutic community: in Air Force Retraining Group, 21, 76, 77, 86; Air Force Treatment Team, 81–83, 86; group discussion in, 83; treatment results, 85–86

Toth: Supreme Court decision on, 5–6

Training, Military, 154, 156

Uniform Code of Military Justice. *See* Military Justice

Unit consultation program, 14

United States Disciplinary Barracks (USDB): established at Rock Island Arsenal, 15; established at Ft. Leavenworth, Kansas, 15; rationale for, 15; history of, 15; policy, 15; description, 16–17; farm, 17; minimum security unit, 17; restoration and clemency review, 17; Special Training Program, 98; offenses of prisoners in, 109; in World War II, 112; evaluation of program in, 112–16, 154, 156; in Korean War, 113–14; post-Korean War program, 114–16. *See also* Rehabilitation; Research Council

Unrest in the Army, 7

Upholstery trade: training for at USDB, 159

Vocational training: post-discharge research on, 21, 172–79; Air Force Educational Service Division in, 80, 82, 83–84, 170–80; London research on, 152; USDB research on, 152–58, 159–69; USDB prisoners preferences for, 154, 156–57; USDB program for, 159; selection criteria for, 159–60; Kansas certification for, 160; post-discharge employment, 165

Wild Beast Test, 145

Wisconsin: insanity in prison, 145

Work: at Ft. Dix, 65, 70–71. *See also* Vocational Training